Better Homes and Gardens®

50 ways to COOK FAST

Our seal assures you that every recipe in *50 Ways to Cook Fast*
has been tested in the Better Homes and Gardens®
Test Kitchen. This means that each recipe is practical and reliable,
and meets our high standards of taste appeal.

BETTER HOMES AND GARDENS® BOOKS
Editor: Gerald M. Knox
Art Director: Ernest Shelton
Managing Editor: David A. Kirchner
Project Editors: James D. Blume, Marsha Jahns
Project Managers: Liz Anderson, Jennifer Speer Ramundt,
   Angela K. Renkoski

Department Head, Cook Books: Sharyl Heiken
Associate Department Heads: Sandra Granseth,
   Rosemary C. Hutchinson, Elizabeth Woolever
Senior Food Editors: Linda Henry, Mary Jo Plutt,
   Joyce Trollope
Associate Food Editors: Jennifer Darling, Debra-Ann Duggan,
   Heather M. Hephner, Mary Major, Shelli McConnell
Test Kitchen: Director, Sharon Stilwell; Photo Studio Director,
   Janet Herwig; Home Economists: Lynn Blanchard, Kay Cargill,
   Marilyn Cornelius, Maryellyn Krantz, Marge Steenson,
   Colleen Weeden

Associate Art Directors: Neoma Thomas, Linda Ford Vermie,
   Randall Yontz
Assistant Art Directors: Lynda Haupert, Harijs Priekulis,
   Tom Wegner
Graphic Designers: Mary Schlueter Bendgen, Michael Burns,
   Brenda Lesch
Art Production: Director, John Berg; Associate, Joe Heuer;
   Office Manager, Michaela Lester

President, Book Group: Jeramy Lanigan
Vice President, Retail Marketing: Jamie Martin
Vice President, Administrative Services: Rick Rundall

BETTER HOMES AND GARDENS® MAGAZINE
President, Magazine Group: James A. Autry
Vice President, Editorial Director: Doris Eby
Food and Nutrition Editor: Nancy Byal

MEREDITH CORPORATE OFFICERS
Chairman of the Executive Committee:
   E. T. Meredith III
Chairman of the Board: Robert A. Burnett
President: Jack D. Rehm

50 WAYS TO COOK FAST
Editor: Linda Henry
Editorial Project Manager: Angela K. Renkoski
Graphic Designer: Lynda Haupert
Electronic Text Processor: Paula Forest
Food Stylists: Lynn Blanchard, Janet Herwig
Contributing Photographer: Scott Little

On the cover: Sweet-and-Sour Chicken Chunks
(see recipe, page 32)

Contents

Great Meals Pronto!

"I don't have time to cook." You hear these words everywhere these days. With time pressures so great, cooking is often squeezed out. But this doesn't have to happen at your house. With the help of *50 Ways to Cook Fast,* you can have delicious meals in the same time it would take you to run to a deli or fast food restaurant.

How? Just select one of our 50 time- and work-saving hints and try it. You'll find multipurpose ideas that work for a variety of recipes—from appetizers to desserts—as well as specific shortcuts that work best for main dishes, side dishes, or desserts. In addition, there are general tips that will help you speed your cooking no matter what recipe you're preparing.

The next time you're about to say "I don't have time to cook," stop and reach for *50 Ways to Cook Fast* instead. You'll be delighted you did.

Start with a jar of spicy salsa instead of mixing together canned tomatoes and additional seasonings.

Shrimp Gumbo

Stir up this Cajun classic in just 10 minutes.

3 cups salsa
1 12-ounce package frozen, peeled, deveined shrimp, rinsed
1 10-ounce package frozen cut okra
1 cup cubed fully cooked ham
¾ to 1 cup water
1 teaspoon instant chicken bouillon granules
2 cups hot cooked rice

◆In a large saucepan stir together salsa, shrimp, okra, ham, water, and chicken bouillon granules.

◆Bring mixture to boiling. Reduce heat and simmer, covered, about 5 minutes or till shrimp turn pink and mixture is heated through. Serve with rice. Makes 4 servings.

Nutrition information per serving: 452 calories, 30 g protein, 69 g carbohydrate, 4 g fat, 148 mg cholesterol, 1,855 mg sodium, 860 mg potassium.

Clam Sauce for Fish

For dinner in a hurry, put frozen breaded fish portions or sticks in the oven, then make this zesty sauce while they bake.

2 tablespoons chopped celery
1 tablespoon margarine *or* butter
1 teaspoon cornstarch
1 cup salsa
1 teaspoon dried parsley flakes
1 6½-ounce can minced clams, drained

◆In a small saucepan cook celery in margarine or butter till tender. Stir in cornstarch. Stir in salsa and parsley. Cook and stir till thickened and bubbly. Cook and stir 2 minutes more. Add clams; cook and stir just till heated through. Serve over poached, broiled, or grilled fish. Store remaining sauce in the refrigerator for up to 4 days. Makes 1⅓ cups.

Nutrition information per tablespoon: 41 calories, 4 g protein, 3 g carbohydrate, 1 g fat, 10 mg cholesterol, 193 mg sodium, 150 mg potassium.

Never-Better Taco Salads

On the table and ready to eat in only 11 minutes!

½ pound ground beef *or* pork
1 8-ounce can red kidney beans, drained
1 cup salsa
4 cups torn mixed greens
½ cup shredded cheddar cheese (2 ounces)
Tortilla chips (about 30)
Frozen avocado dip, thawed (optional)
Dairy sour cream (optional)

◆In a medium saucepan cook ground beef or pork till browned. Drain off fat. Stir in kidney beans and salsa.

◆Bring meat mixture to boiling. Reduce heat. Simmer, uncovered, about 5 minutes or till of desired consistency.

◆Meanwhile, arrange greens on dinner plates. Spoon meat mixture atop greens. Sprinkle with shredded cheese. Arrange tortilla chips around edges of plates. Serve with avocado dip and sour cream, if desired. Makes 3 or 4 servings.

Nutrition information per serving: 458 calories, 25 g protein, 35 g carbohydrate, 23 g fat, 71 mg cholesterol, 894 mg sodium, 663 mg potassium.

Bloody Marys

You're gonna love our quick-to-fix, slushy version of this classic cocktail.

1 12-ounce jar salsa
½ teaspoon seasoned salt
20 to 24 ice cubes (about 3 cups)
½ cup vodka
4 lemon *or* lime wedges

◆In a blender container combine salsa and seasoned salt. Cover and blend till smooth. Add ice and vodka. Cover and blend till slushy. Garnish each serving with lemon or lime wedges. Makes 4 (8-ounce) servings.

Nutrition information per serving: 105 calories, 0 g protein, 6 g carbohydrate, 0 g fat, 0 mg cholesterol, 773 mg sodium, 187 mg potassium.

Never-Better Taco Salads

From sandwiches to desserts, you can speed preparation by starting with a packaged or frozen breakfast item.

Mock Monte Cristo Sandwiches

Usually Monte Cristo sandwiches are dipped in egg and milk before cooking. By starting with frozen French toast, our shortcut version eliminates that messy step.

3 **ounces sliced fully cooked turkey breast**
3 **ounces sliced fully cooked ham**
3 **ounces thinly sliced Swiss cheese**
6 **slices frozen French toast**

◆ To assemble sandwiches, layer turkey, ham, and cheese atop *3* slices of the frozen French toast. Top with remaining frozen French toast.

◆ Place sandwiches on a baking sheet. Bake in a 400° oven for 20 to 25 minutes or till sandwiches are heated through; turn sandwiches over once. Makes 3 servings.

Nutrition information per serving: 295 calories, 24 g protein, 22 g carbohydrate, 12 g fat, 189 mg cholesterol, 562 mg sodium, 265 mg potassium.

Croissant Shortcakes

Thawed fruit also works well in this easy-to-fix dessert.

4 **bakery *or* frozen croissants**
1½ **cups fresh raspberries, strawberries, blueberries, *or* mixed fruit**
½ **cup red raspberry *or* apricot preserves, *or* strawberry *or* currant jelly**
Pressurized whipped dessert topping

◆ Heat bakery croissants in a 350° oven for 5 minutes. (*Or,* heat frozen croissants according to package directions.) Let cool 5 minutes; carefully split lengthwise.

◆ Meanwhile, in a medium bowl stir together fruit and preserves or jelly. Pair raspberries, strawberries, or blueberries with the raspberry preserves or strawberry or currant jelly. Pair the mixed fruit with the apricot preserves.

◆ Spread croissant bottoms with some of the fruit mixture and a little dessert topping. Replace croissant tops. Top with remaining fruit mixture and dessert topping. Makes 4 servings.

Nutrition information per serving: 319 calories, 5 g protein, 52 g carbohydrate, 11 g fat, 0 mg cholesterol, 143 mg sodium, 157 mg potassium.

Make quick work of chores such as chopping, snipping, shredding, wedging, and slicing with these smooth tricks.

Make quick work of snipping parsley, basil, dill, or other fresh herbs by placing the leaves in a 1-cup glass measure. Then, snip them finely with kitchen shears.

Kitchen shears also come in handy for cutting up canned tomatoes. Just snip the tomatoes right in the can, and you're all set to use them in soups, stews, or casseroles.

If you've always thought shredding lettuce for tacos or sandwiches was a chore, try this handy tip. First, cut a wedge of iceberg lettuce. (You should get about 3 cups shredded lettuce from a quarter-head.) Place the wedge on a cutting board. Holding it with one hand, use a long-bladed knife to cut the lettuce into ¼-inch strips.

There are lots of gadgets for speeding up chores in the kitchen. Keep these in mind to help with slicing or making wedges: a tomato slicer, an egg slicer or wedger, an apple wedger.

Chopping onions is no work at all if you first cut them in half. Then, place one half cut-side-down on a cutting board. Slice the onion half in one direction. Next, holding the slices together, slice at a 90-degree angle to the first cuts. Repeat with the other onion half. Use this tip for carrots or potatoes, too.

Coleslaw is a breeze if you use your blender to chop the cabbage. First, rinse the cabbage. Then, cut it into wedges, removing the core. Place a few wedges at a time into your blender container. Cover the wedges with cold water. Cover the blender container. Running the blender with an on-and-off motion, blend the cabbage just till it's coarsely chopped. Drain the cabbage well. Try this for carrots, celery, sweet pepper, and onion, too.

For julienne strips in no time, cut food into slices 2 inches long and ¼ to ½ inch thick. Stack the slices and cut lengthwise into matchstick-size pieces.

Open jars of fruit and vegetable baby food instead of cooking and pureeing fresh produce.

Fruit-Filled Coffee Cake

For sour milk, add 1½ teaspoons lemon juice or vinegar to enough milk to make ½ cup.

¾ cup sugar
1½ cups all-purpose flour
½ teaspoon baking powder
¼ teaspoon baking soda
6 tablespoons margarine
    or butter
1 beaten egg
½ cup buttermilk *or* sour
    milk
½ teaspoon vanilla
3 4½-ounce jars strained
    apricot *or* peach baby
    food
¼ cup all-purpose flour

◆In a mixing bowl stir together *½ cup* of the sugar, the 1½ cups flour, baking powder, and baking soda. Cut in *4 tablespoons* of the margarine or butter till mixture resembles fine crumbs.

◆In a small bowl combine egg, buttermilk or sour milk, and vanilla. Add to flour mixture. Stir just till moistened. Spread *half* of the batter into a greased 8x8x2-inch baking pan.

◆Spread fruit baby food over batter in baking pan. Drop remaining batter in small mounds atop fruit.

◆Combine the remaining sugar and the ¼ cup flour. Cut in remaining margarine or butter till mixture resembles fine crumbs. Sprinkle over batter. Bake in a 350° oven for 40 to 45 minutes or till golden brown. Serve warm. Makes 9 servings.

Nutrition information per serving: 261 calories, 4 g protein, 43 g carbohydrate, 9 g fat, 31 mg cholesterol, 163 mg sodium, 107 mg potassium.

Barbecue Sauce

A great family-style barbecue sauce—not too hot, not too sweet.

1 4½-ounce jar strained
   apricot, pear with
   pineapple, *or* peach baby
   food
⅓ cup catsup
2 tablespoons vinegar
1 tablespoon brown sugar
   (optional)
1 teaspoon Worcestershire
   sauce
   Dash bottled hot pepper
   sauce

◆In a small saucepan stir together fruit baby food; catsup; vinegar; brown sugar, if desired; Worcestershire sauce; and bottled hot pepper sauce. Simmer, uncovered, about 5 minutes or till sauce reaches desired consistency. Serve over burgers or poultry. Makes about ¾ cup.

Nutrition information per tablespoon: 15 calories, 0 g protein, 4 g carbohydrate, 0 g fat, 0 mg cholesterol, 85 mg sodium, 43 mg potassium.

Creamy Carrot Soup

For a touch of elegance, swirl sour cream or yogurt into this rich, delicate-flavored soup.

2 cups light cream *or* milk
4 teaspoons all-purpose flour
2 6-ounce jars junior carrot
   baby food
1½ teaspoons instant chicken
   bouillon granules
½ teaspoon curry powder *or*
   ¼ teaspoon dried
   dillweed
⅛ teaspoon onion salt
⅛ teaspoon pepper

◆In a medium saucepan stir together cream or milk, and flour. Stir in carrot baby food, chicken bouillon granules, curry powder or dillweed, onion salt, and pepper. Cook and stir over medium-high heat till thickened and bubbly. Cook and stir for 1 minute more. Makes 4 side-dish servings.

Nutrition information per serving: 268 calories, 4 g protein, 12 g carbohydrate, 23 g fat, 79 mg cholesterol, 269 mg sodium, 321 mg potassium.

Oven-fry rather than deep-fry crispy potato slices or chicken pieces for less mess and no fuss.

Oven-Fried Potatoes

These flavor-packed potatoes go great with grilled poultry, steaks, chops, or burgers.

2 medium potatoes,
   bias-sliced about
   ¼ inch thick
2 tablespoons melted
   margarine *or* butter
   or cooking oil
¼ teaspoon garlic powder
¼ teaspoon dried basil,
   oregano, *or* thyme,
   crushed; *or* dillweed
⅛ teaspoon pepper
2 tablespoons grated
   Parmesan *or* Romano
   cheese (optional)

◆ Scrub potatoes; do not peel. Stir together margarine, butter, or oil; garlic powder; desired herb; and pepper. Place potato slices in a single layer on the unheated rack of a broiler pan. Brush margarine mixture over both sides of potato slices. Broil about 5 inches from the heat for 8 to 9 minutes or till potatoes begin to brown.

◆ Using a wide spatula, turn potatoes over. Broil for 4 to 6 minutes more or till potatoes are tender. Sprinkle with cheese, if desired. Makes 4 servings.

Nutrition information per serving: 145 calories, 2 g protein, 22 g carbohydrate, 6 g fat, 0 mg cholesterol, 74 mg sodium, 364 mg potassium.

Turning slices with ease
Using a wide spatula will help you turn the potato slices without breaking them. Once you have the slices flipped, broil them 4 to 6 minutes more or until they are tender when you test them with a fork. For extra flavor punch, sprinkle the hot slices with grated Parmesan cheese right before serving.

Almost as easy as take-out chicken—with a delightful, home-cooked flavor and less fat.

2 tablespoons margarine *or*
  butter
4 boned skinless medium
  chicken breast halves
  (about 1 pound total) *or*
  8 chicken thighs, skinned
  (about 2½ pounds)
1 cup corn bread *or* herb-
  seasoned stuffing mix *or*
  cornflakes, coarsely
  crushed

◆ Set oven to 375°. Place margarine in a shallow baking pan; place in oven for 3 to 4 minutes or till margarine melts.

◆ Meanwhile, rinse chicken; pat dry. Dip chicken pieces into melted margarine; then roll in stuffing mix or cornflakes to coat. Place chicken pieces atop remaining melted margarine in the pan. Bake in a 375° oven 20 to 25 minutes for breasts or 35 to 45 minutes for thighs, or till tender and no longer pink. Makes 4 servings.

Nutrition information per serving: 321 calories, 31 g protein, 25 g carbohydrate, 10 g fat, 74 mg cholesterol, 596 mg sodium, 281 mg potassium.

Coating chicken pieces
To quickly coat the chicken breast halves, place the crushed corn bread, herb-seasoned stuffing mix, or cornflakes into a shallow bowl or pie plate. First, dip the chicken breast halves in the melted margarine or butter, then roll them in the crushed mixture.

Deli-Vegetable Sandwich

Three-Bean-Plus Salad

Oh-So-Easy Deli Salad
(see recipe, page 16)

Take advantage of work-saving ingredients from a delicatessen to make these easy-on-the-cook salads and sandwiches.

Deli-Vegetable Sandwich

Deliciously different and ready in minutes when you use cooked meat, marinated salad, and cheese from the deli.

4 **French-style rolls (about 6 inches long)**
3 **tablespoons coarse-grain brown mustard *or* Dijon-style mustard**
8 **ounces thinly sliced cooked beef, turkey, *or* ham**
1 **pint (2 cups) delicatessen marinated mixed vegetable salad, drained**
4 **ounces thinly sliced Swiss, provolone, brick, *or* creamy Havarti cheese**

◆ Cut a thin slice off the top of each roll. Hollow out bottoms, leaving about a ½-inch shell (save bread for crumbs). Spread the inside of *each* roll shell with about *2 teaspoons* mustard.

◆ Pile desired sliced meat inside roll shells. Fill each with vegetable salad and top with desired cheese.

◆ If desired, place on the unheated rack of a broiler pan. Broil about 4 inches from heat for 1 to 2 minutes or till cheese begins to melt. Cover with roll tops. Makes 4 servings.

Nutrition information per serving: 425 calories, 32 g protein, 35 g carbohydrate, 17 g fat, 82 mg cholesterol, 495 mg sodium, 431 mg potassium.

Three-Bean-Plus Salad

If you're using the canned salad, get a head start by chilling it in the refrigerator overnight.

1½ **cups wagon wheel *or* corkscrew macaroni**
1 **pint (2 cups) delicatessen three-bean salad *or* one 15- *or* 17-ounce can three-bean salad**
1 **6-ounce package sliced turkey luncheon meat *or* sliced fully cooked ham, cut into bite-size strips**
1 **cup cubed American, cheddar, *or* Swiss cheese (4 ounces)**
4 **lettuce leaves (optional)**

◆ Cook the macaroni according to package directions; drain. Transfer cooked macaroni to a bowl of ice water. Let stand for 5 minutes. Drain well.

◆ Meanwhile, in a large bowl combine *undrained* three-bean salad, turkey or ham strips, and cubed cheese. Add macaroni. Toss till well-coated.

◆ Chill salad in freezer for 15 minutes. If desired, serve on lettuce-lined plates. Makes 4 main-dish or 8 side-dish servings.

Nutrition information per main-dish serving: 373 calories, 25 g protein, 41 g carbohydrate, 12 g fat, 59 mg cholesterol, 927 mg sodium, 376 mg potassium.

Oh-So-Easy Deli Salad

Salad bars offer you a variety of vegetables, plus they save you the time and trouble of cleaning and cutting your choices (pictured on page 14).

1 cup medium shell *or* elbow macaroni

3 cups cut-up, salad-bar vegetables (broccoli flowerets, cauliflower flowerets, sliced radishes, carrots, green pepper rings *or* strips, cucumber slices, fresh mushrooms, cherry tomatoes, *or* zucchini slices)

⅓ cup creamy buttermilk *or* creamy Italian salad dressing

Lettuce leaves (optional)

◆ Cook macaroni according to package directions; drain. Transfer cooked macaroni to a bowl of ice water. Let stand for 5 minutes. Drain well.

◆ Meanwhile, cut up any large salad-bar vegetables, if necessary. In a large bowl combine vegetables and salad dressing. Add macaroni. Toss till well-coated.

◆ Chill salad in freezer for 15 minutes. If desired, serve on lettuce-lined salad plates. Makes 4 servings.

Nutrition information per serving: 216 calories, 5 g protein, 31 g carbohydrate, 8 g fat, 1 mg cholesterol, 176 mg sodium, 286 mg potassium.

Stock your kitchen shelves and refrigerator with work-saving ingredients to speed meal preparation.

These timesaving items may sometimes cost a bit more, but their convenience may make them worth every penny.

◆

Dairy Items:
 Shredded or sliced cheeses
 Flavored sour-cream dips
 Soft-style cream cheese
 Grated Parmesan or Romano cheese

◆

Meats:
 Cooked meats from the deli
 Canned ham
 Cooked bacon pieces

◆

Poultry:
 (see tip box, page 37)
 Canned chicken
 Canned turkey

◆

Fish and Seafood:
 (see tip box, page 46)

◆

Vegetables:
 Bottled minced garlic
 Dried minced onion
 Dried parsley flakes
 Frozen chopped onion
 Frozen chopped green pepper
 Shredded cabbage or coleslaw mixes

◆

Herb and Spice Blends:
 Italian seasoning
 Curry powder
 Five-spice powder
 Chili powder
 Poultry seasoning
 Pumpkin pie spice

◆

Miscellaneous Items:
 Bread crumbs and croutons
 Broken, chopped, or ground nuts
 Flaked, shredded, or grated coconut
 Crushed graham crackers
 Refrigerated pie or pizza crust

Cut your measuring and mixing time by using a handy packaged biscuit mix to create appetizers or desserts.

Tex-Mex Appetizer Rounds

If you love nachos piled high with goodies, these mini-pizzas are right up your alley.

2 cups packaged biscuit mix
1 8-ounce carton dairy sour cream
1 9- *or* 10-ounce can jalapeño bean dip
⅓ cup taco sauce
1 cup shredded Monterey Jack *or* cheddar cheese
¼ cup chopped pitted ripe olives
  Frozen avocado dip, thawed (optional)

◆ In a mixing bowl combine biscuit mix and sour cream; beat vigorously till moistened. On a lightly floured surface knead dough 20 times. Roll dough to ¼-inch thickness. Cut with a floured 2-inch round cutter. Place cutouts on two ungreased baking sheets.

◆ For filling, stir together bean dip and taco sauce. Set aside.

◆ With floured fingertips, make a deep indentation about 1½ inches in diameter in center of each dough round. Fill *each* indentation with a *heaping teaspoon* of bean dip mixture; spread inside indentation.

◆ Top each dough round with cheese and olives. Bake in a 400° oven for 10 to 12 minutes or till lightly browned. Top each with avocado dip, if desired. Makes 30.

Nutrition information per appetizer: 75 calories, 2 g protein, 7 g carbohydrate, 4 g fat, 7 mg cholesterol, 187 mg sodium, 58 mg potassium.

Easy Pear Dumplings

Easy enough for anytime, elegant enough for special occasions.

⅓ cup apricot preserves
3 tablespoons chopped walnuts
1 cup water
⅓ cup sugar
2 tablespoons brown sugar
½ teaspoon ground cinnamon
2 tablespoons margarine *or* butter
½ teaspoon vanilla
1⅓ cup packaged biscuit mix
⅓ cup milk
1 tablespoon sugar
1 tablespoon margarine *or* butter, melted
6 small pears, peeled and cored

◆ In a mixing bowl combine preserves and walnuts. Set aside.

◆ For syrup, in a saucepan combine water, the ⅓ cup sugar, brown sugar, and cinnamon. Cook and stir over medium heat till sugar is dissolved. Stir in the 2 tablespoons margarine or butter and the vanilla. Set aside.

◆ For pastry, combine biscuit mix, milk, the 1 tablespoon sugar, and the 1 tablespoon margarine; stir till moistened. Knead gently on a well-floured surface 8 to 10 strokes. Roll into a 12x8-inch rectangle. Cut into six 4-inch squares.

◆ Place syrup in a 12x7½x2-inch baking dish. Add pears. Fill center of each pear with some of the preserves mixture.

◆ Carefully place one dough square over each pear. Cut a small crisscross in dough on top of each pear (or cut out a design in center of square with a small cutter before placing on pear). Bake in a 375° oven about 40 minutes or till pears are tender. Cover loosely with foil the last 10 to 15 minutes of baking to prevent overbrowning. Serve warm. Makes 6 servings.

Nutrition information per serving: 373 calories, 3 g protein, 66 g carbohydrate, 13 g fat, 4 mg cholesterol, 311 mg sodium, 283 mg potassium.

Topping pears
To finish the dumplings, top each pear with a dough square. Then, carefully cut a crisscross in the center of the square. If you like, use a small cookie or canape cutter to cut a design in each dough square before you place it on top of the pear.

Shorten the cooking time of slow-baking main dishes and desserts by preparing them on the range top instead of in the oven.

Macaroni and Four-Cheese Special

This is no ordinary macaroni and cheese. It's spiffed up with tricolored pasta, garlic, Dijon-style mustard, and four cheeses—cream, cheddar, mozzarella, and Parmesan.

2½ cups tricolored spiral
    or elbow macaroni
½ cup chopped onion
2 cloves garlic, minced
2 tablespoons margarine
    or butter
1 tablespoon all-purpose
    flour
1½ cups milk
1 4-ounce package shredded
    mozzarella cheese
    (1 cup)
1 4-ounce package shredded
    cheddar cheese (1 cup)
1 3-ounce package cream
    cheese, cut up
1 tablespoon Dijon-style *or*
    stone-ground mustard
¼ teaspoon pepper
2 tablespoons grated
    Parmesan cheese

◆ In large saucepan cook pasta in boiling *unsalted* water till barely tender. Drain.

◆ Meanwhile, in a medium saucepan cook onion and garlic in margarine or butter till tender but not brown. Stir in flour. Add milk all at once. Cook and stir till slightly thickened and bubbly.

◆ Stir in mozzarella cheese, cheddar cheese, and cream cheese. Cook and stir over low heat till cheese melts. Stir in Dijon-style or stone-ground mustard and pepper.

◆ Stir pasta into cheese sauce. Heat through. Sprinkle with Parmesan and serve immediately. Makes 6 main-dish servings.

Nutrition information per serving: 394 calories, 18 g protein, 33 g carbohydrate, 21 g fat, 51 mg cholesterol, 441 mg sodium, 250 mg potassium.

No-Bake Cookies

Try these tasty cookies when you need a project to cure the kids of the "I'm bored" blues.

2 cups sugar
½ cup margarine *or* butter
½ cup milk
2 tablespoons unsweetened
    cocoa powder
½ cup chunky peanut butter
1 teaspoon vanilla
¼ teaspoon ground cinnamon
3 cups quick-cooking
    rolled oats

◆ In a heavy 2-quart saucepan stir together sugar, margarine or butter, milk, and cocoa powder. Bring to full boil over medium heat; boil for 1 minute, stirring occasionally.

◆ Remove from heat and stir in peanut butter, vanilla, and cinnamon. Add oats. Beat with wooden spoon 2 to 3 minutes or till mixture just begins to set. Immediately drop by rounded teaspoonfuls onto a cookie sheet lined with waxed paper. Cool. Makes about 40 cookies.

Nutrition information per serving: 130 calories, 2 g protein, 15 g carbohydrate, 4 g fat, 0 mg cholesterol, 46 mg sodium, 51 mg potassium.

Oh-so-good served with a dab of whipped cream or ice cream.

2 tablespoons raisins,
   currants, snipped pitted
   dates, *or* dried mixed
   fruit bits
2 tablespoons finely chopped
   walnuts *or* pecans
1 tablespoon brown sugar
¼ teaspoon ground cinnamon
¾ cup apple juice
1 tablespoon sugar
4 small cooking apples

For filling, combine raisins, currants, dates, or fruit bits; nuts; brown sugar; and cinnamon. Set aside.

In a large saucepan combine apple juice and sugar. Set aside.

Remove core and a strip of peel from the top of each apple. Stuff center of each apple with filling and place in the saucepan.

Bring mixture to boiling. Reduce heat and simmer, covered, for 15 minutes or till apples are tender when tested with a fork.

To serve, spoon apples and some of the juice into dessert dishes. Makes 4 servings.

Nutrition information per serving: 151 calories, 1 g protein, 33 g carbohydrate, 3 g fat, 0 mg cholesterol, 3 mg sodium, 250 mg potassium.

Perfectly baked apples
The secret to tender, juicy apples is to use a saucepan with a tight-fitting lid that is deep enough to hold the apples. This way the apples can cook without the tops drying out.

Grab ready-to-use pasta and sauce products in the grocery store for a head start on fantastic recipe ideas.

If you yearn for pasta but don't have the time to make it from scratch, try one of our minute-saving methods.

◆

Turn bottled or refrigerated tomato-based spaghetti sauces into main dishes by adding cooked ground beef or pork, cooked Italian sausage links, or canned minced clams. Just be sure to drain the meat or clams well before you add them to the sauce to heat.

◆

Make a quick, but elegant, primavera sauce by tossing together heated refrigerated Alfredo sauce and a cup or so of cooked vegetables. Then serve over hot cooked linguine or fettuccine.

◆

For another fancy pasta fix-up, stir canned or cooked, frozen shrimp into heated refrigerated Alfredo or marinara sauce. Serve the sauce over your favorite pasta and sprinkle it with grated Parmesan or Romano cheese.

Concoct an easy pasta salad by combining cooked tortellini, some re-frigerated pesto sauce, and your favorite cooked vegetables. Then chill and serve. If you're really in a hurry, place the salad in the freezer for 20 minutes. For a creamy version, use mayonnaise or salad dressing in place of the pesto.

◆

When you need a side dish to round out a menu, toss some cooked pasta with some melted margarine or butter seasoned with dried basil or dillweed, snipped chives, or minced garlic.

◆

When every minute counts, rely on refrigerated pasta products rather than frozen or dried versions, because they cook faster. You also can speed up cooking by using less water to cook the pasta. Four cups of water is enough to cook up to 7 or 8 ounces of pasta.

Shave minutes from cooking time by preparing small, individual portions of food.

Pork Mini-Loaves

Home-style meatloaf... just as good as ever... only smaller.

3 tablespoons chutney
1 beaten egg
¼ cup fine dry bread crumbs
2 tablespoons raisins
1 tablespoon dried minced
   onion
1 teaspoon prepared mustard
½ teaspoon salt
⅛ teaspoon pepper
1 pound ground pork *or*
   beef
   Chutney (optional)

◆ Snip any large pieces of chutney; set aside. In a medium mixing bowl combine the beaten egg and the 3 tablespoons chutney. Stir in bread crumbs, raisins, onion, mustard, salt, and pepper. Add ground pork or beef, and mix well.

◆ Shape meat mixture into four 4x2-inch loaves. Place in a 10x6x2-inch baking dish. Bake, uncovered, in a 350° oven for 35 to 40 minutes or till meat is well done.

◆ Transfer loaves to a serving platter. Serve with additional chutney, if desired. Makes 4 servings.

Nutrition information per serving: 300 calories, 27 g protein, 17 g carbohydrate, 13 g fat, 152 mg cholesterol, 427 mg sodium, 479 mg potassium.

Individual Brownie Soufflés

Few desserts are as tempting as this flourless chocolate creation.

4 eggs
⅓ cup milk
¼ cup sugar
1 teaspoon vanilla
¼ teaspoon ground cinnamon
1 8-ounce package cream
   cheese, cut up
1 5½-ounce can (½ cup)
   chocolate-flavored
   syrup
2 teaspoons powdered sugar

◆ In a blender container or food processor bowl combine eggs, milk, sugar, vanilla, and cinnamon. Cover, and blend or process till smooth. With blender or food processor running, add cream cheese pieces, blending till smooth.

◆ Add the chocolate syrup. Cover, and blend or process till combined. Pour mixture into four 1-cup soufflé dishes.

◆ Bake in a 375° oven for 30 to 35 minutes or till a knife inserted near the center comes out clean. *Quickly* sprinkle tops with powdered sugar. Serve immediately. Makes 4 servings.

Nutrition information per serving: 436 calories, 12 g protein, 41 g carbohydrate, 27 g fat, 339 mg cholesterol, 268 mg sodium, 275 mg potassium.

**Deep, Deep-Dish
Spinach Pizza**

Save lots of work as well as dishwashing drudgery with these next two family-pleasing one-dish meals.

Deep, Deep-Dish Spinach Pizza

1 16-ounce package hot roll mix
1 pound ground beef *or* ground raw turkey
1 cup chopped onion
1 clove garlic, minced
1 8-ounce can pizza sauce
1 3-ounce package sliced pepperoni
1 2-ounce can mushrooms, drained
¼ cup sliced pitted ripe olives
1 teaspoon Italian seasoning, crushed
¼ teaspoon crushed red pepper
1½ cups shredded mozzarella cheese
1 10-ounce package frozen chopped spinach, thawed and drained well
1 slightly beaten egg

◈ Prepare hot roll mix through the kneading step in the basic recipe directions on the package. Cover and let rest.

◈ Meanwhile, in a large skillet cook beef or turkey, onion, and garlic till meat is brown and onion is tender. Drain off fat. Stir in pizza sauce, pepperoni, mushrooms, olives, Italian seasoning, and red pepper. Cook till heated through; cover and keep warm.

◈ On a lightly floured surface roll *three-fourths* of the dough into a 13-inch circle. Fit into bottom and press up sides of a 9-inch springform pan. Sprinkle bottom of dough with ½ *cup* of the mozzarella cheese. Spoon meat mixture over cheese.

◈ Pat spinach dry with paper towels. Combine spinach, egg, and remaining mozzarella cheese. Spread spinach mixture over meat mixture.

◈ Roll remaining dough into a 9-inch circle; place atop spinach. Fold excess bottom dough under; pinch to seal.

◈ Bake in a 350° oven for 40 to 45 minutes. Cool 10 minutes on a wire rack. To serve, remove sides of springform pan; cut into wedges. Makes 8 servings.

Nutrition information per serving: 514 calories, 27 g protein, 50 g carbohydrate, 22 g fat, 124 mg cholesterol, 1,065 mg sodium, 523 mg potassium.

Sealing the edges
Once you have topped the filling with the 9-inch dough circle, fold the excess dough under. Then pinch the edges together, making a decorative border.

Skillet Enchiladas

Truly a fiesta in a skillet.

½ pound ground beef
½ cup chopped onion
1 11-ounce can enchilada
  sauce
1 10¾-ounce can condensed
  cream of mushroom
  soup
⅓ cup milk
1 4-ounce can diced green
  chili peppers
1½ cups shredded cheddar
  cheese (10 ounces)
1 cup shredded carrot
3 tablespoons cooking oil
10 6-inch corn tortillas
1 8-ounce can red kidney
  beans, drained and
  slightly mashed
½ cup chopped pitted ripe
  olives (optional)
  Sour cream *or* guacamole
  (optional)

◆ For sauce, in a 12-inch skillet cook ground beef and onion till meat is brown and onion is tender. Drain off fat. Stir in enchilada sauce, soup, milk, and chili peppers. Bring to boiling; reduce heat. Simmer, covered, for 10 minutes.

◆ Meanwhile, set aside ⅓ *cup* of the cheese. Stir together remaining cheese and carrot; set aside. In a heavy medium skillet heat oil. Dip tortillas, one at a time, in hot oil for 10 seconds or just till limp. Drain on paper towels. (Or, omit oil and wrap tortillas in microwave-safe plastic wrap. Micro-cook on 100% power [high] for 1 minute or till softened.)

◆ Spread some of the beans down the center of each tortilla. Place a scant ¼ *cup* of the cheese mixture on *each* tortilla; sprinkle with olives, if desired. Roll up tortillas and place in sauce in the skillet. Cover and cook about 5 minutes or till heated through. Sprinkle with reserved ⅓ cup cheese. Serve with sour cream or guacamole, if desired. Makes 5 servings.

Nutrition information per serving: 709 calories, 34 g protein, 35 g carbohydrate, 48 g fat, 122 mg cholesterol, 1,689 mg sodium, 508 mg potassium.

Adding the cheese
Top this easy one-dish meal with a generous sprinkling of cheddar cheese. Then serve the enchiladas with your choice of sour cream or guacamole or both.

Skip the work and mess of pounding chicken breast halves by using turkey breast slices or cutlets.

Turkey Roulade

This easy recipe with its zesty cranberry glaze will remind you of Thanksgiving dinner at Grandma's house.

1 8-ounce can whole-berry cranberry sauce
¼ cup bottled barbecue sauce
4 turkey breast tenderloin steaks (about 1 pound)
1 medium green pepper, cut into strips

◆In a small saucepan stir together cranberry sauce and barbecue sauce. Brush one side of each turkey breast steak with some of the sauce mixture. Place several green pepper strips crosswise on the sauced side of each turkey breast steak. Roll up jelly-roll style from one short side; secure bundles with wooden toothpicks.

◆Place turkey bundles, seam side down, in an ungreased 8x8x1½-inch baking dish. Bake, uncovered, in a 375° oven about 25 minutes or till turkey is no longer pink.

◆Meanwhile, cook remaining sauce mixture over low heat till heated through. Spoon over turkey bundles. Makes 4 servings.

Nutrition information per serving: 217 calories, 26 g protein, 25 g carbohydrate, 1 g fat, 71 mg cholesterol, 189 mg sodium, 326 mg potassium.

Salmon Salad Niçoise

Use bottled salad dressing for a quick marinade instead of combining cooking oil, vinegar, and seasonings.

Salmon Salad Niçoise

1 16-ounce can sliced
  potatoes, drained, *or* one
  16-ounce can whole white
  potatoes, drained
1 cup frozen cut green beans
¼ cup pitted ripe olives
½ of a small red onion, sliced
  and separated into rings
1 8-ounce bottle Italian salad
  dressing
1 medium tomato, sliced
2 6½-ounce cans skinless
  boneless salmon *or*
  chunk white tuna (water-
  pack), drained
  Lettuce leaves
1 hard-cooked egg, sliced

◆ If using whole potatoes, cut them into bite-size pieces. In a large bowl combine potatoes, green beans, olives, and onion slices. Pour salad dressing over all.

◆ Halve tomato slices. Gently stir salmon or tuna, and tomatoes into potato mixture. Cover and marinate in refrigerator for 2 to 24 hours, stirring once or twice.

◆ To serve, use a slotted spoon to transfer salad mixture to a lettuce-lined plate. Garnish with sliced egg. Makes 4 servings.

Nutrition information per serving: 369 calories, 20 g protein, 17 g carbohydrate, 25 g fat, 96 mg cholesterol, 535 mg sodium, 620 mg potassium.

Marinated Flank Steak

1 pound beef flank steak
½ cup Spices-and-Herbs salad
  dressing
½ teaspoon bottled minced
  garlic *or* ¼ teaspoon
  garlic powder
¼ to ½ teaspoon coarsely
  cracked black pepper
¼ teaspoon onion powder

◆ Score the flank steak by making shallow cuts at 1-inch intervals diagonally across the steak in a diamond pattern. Repeat on second side. Place meat in a plastic bag.

◆ For marinade, combine salad dressing, garlic, pepper, and onion powder. Pour marinade over meat. Close bag. Marinate in refrigerator for 4 to 24 hours, turning bag occasionally.

◆ Remove meat from bag, reserving marinade. Place meat on the unheated rack of a broiler pan. Broil 3 inches from the heat for 6 minutes; brush with marinade. Turn and brush with marinade. Broil for 5 to 6 minutes more for rare or 7 to 8 minutes more for medium-rare. To serve, thinly slice diagonally across the grain. Makes 4 servings.

Nutrition information per serving: 346 calories, 22 g protein, 3 g carbohydrate, 27 g fat, 60 mg cholesterol, 302 mg sodium, 355 mg potassium.

Shape ground meat quickly into meatballs of the same size with one of these three foolproof methods.

Shaping meatballs so they are nicely rounded and all the same size can be a time-consuming chore. But if you use one of these work-savers, you can shape dozens of meatballs in just minutes.

Shaping 1-inch meatballs is a snap if you start by patting the meat mixture into a 1-inch-thick square or rectangle on waxed paper. Then, cut the meat mixture into 1-inch cubes and roll each cube into a ball. If you want 2-inch meatballs, pat the meat mixture into a 2-inch-thick square or rectangle and cut it into 2-inch cubes.

Slicing meatballs is slick, too. First shape the meat mixture into a log the same diameter as the size meatball you need. For 1-inch meatballs, you'll be working with a 1-inch-diameter log. Then, slice the roll into even pieces. Finally, round the pieces into balls.

Scoops can save you time when shaping meatballs. A ¼-cup capacity ice-cream scoop is great for 1½- to 2-inch meatballs, a 1- or 2-tablespoon capacity ice-cream scoop is best for 1-inch meatballs, and a melon baller is perfect for ½-inch size. Simply roll each scoopful of meat into a ball.

Other Meatball Timesavers:
1) To keep the meat mixture from sticking to your hands, rinse your hands with cold water before you start shaping the meatballs.
2) Baking meatballs in the oven rather than frying them in a skillet saves both time and mess. For 1-inch beef or pork meatballs, bake them in a shallow baking pan in a 375° oven about 20 minutes or until no pink remains.

Create a rich and creamy cheese sauce in a hurry by starting with a work-saving soft cheese spread.

Creamy Sausage and Tortellini

For a change of pace, try different cream-cheese flavors.

1 cup cheese-filled tortellini
    (4 ounces)
2 cups broccoli flowerets
½ pound smoked Polish
    sausage *or* fully cooked
    bratwurst, sliced
1 8-ounce container soft-style
    cream cheese with chives
    and onion
1 tablespoon coarse-grain
    brown mustard

◆ In a large saucepan cook tortellini according to package directions, *except* add broccoli flowerets, and Polish sausage or bratwurst slices the last 5 minutes of cooking; stir occasionally.

◆ Drain tortellini mixture; return to hot pan. Stir in soft-style cream cheese and mustard till cheese melts. Makes 4 servings.

Nutrition information per serving: 464 calories, 18 g protein, 13 g carbohydrate, 38 g fat, 74 mg cholesterol, 808 mg sodium, 382 mg potassium.

Easy Salmon Melts

This cheesy, kid-pleasing sandwich calls for a knife and fork.

1 5-ounce jar American
    cheese spread
¼ cup mayonnaise *or* salad
    dressing
1 6½-ounce can skinless,
    boneless salmon *or* one
    6½-ounce can tuna,
    drained and broken into
    chunks
½ cup finely chopped celery
1 teaspoon lemon juice
½ teaspoon dried dillweed
3 English muffins, split and
    toasted

◆ In a medium mixing bowl combine *half* of the cheese spread (about ⅓ cup), and the mayonnaise or salad dressing. Stir in salmon or tuna, celery, lemon juice, and dillweed.

◆ Spread salmon or tuna mixture over English muffin halves. Place muffins on the unheated rack of a broiler pan. Broil 4 inches from the heat for about 3 minutes or till heated through.

◆ Top each with a dollop of the remaining cheese spread. Broil 30 to 60 seconds more or till cheese melts. Makes 3 servings.

Nutrition information per serving: 519 calories, 26 g protein, 37 g carbohydrate, 30 g fat, 55 mg cholesterol, 784 mg sodium, 388 mg potassium.

17 *Try frozen breaded chicken chunks instead of taking the time to bread and deep-fat fry regular chicken pieces.*

Sweet-and-Sour Chicken Chunks

Five ingredients and fast! (Also pictured on the cover.)

1 10-ounce package frozen breaded small chunk-shape chicken patties
1 cup quick-cooking rice
1 16-ounce can unpeeled apricot halves, drained
1 8- to 10-ounce jar sweet-and-sour sauce
1 6-ounce package frozen pea pods

◆ Bake chicken chunks according to package directions.

◆ Meanwhile, in a medium saucepan bring 1 cup *water* to boiling. Stir in rice. Remove pan from heat. Cover and let stand for 5 minutes.

◆ In a saucepan mix the apricots, sweet-and-sour sauce, and pea pods. Cook and stir till mixture is heated through.

◆ To serve, spoon rice on a platter. Arrange chicken over rice around the edge of the platter. Spoon apricot mixture into the center of the chicken. Makes 4 servings.

Nutrition information per serving: 320 calories, 15 g protein, 40 g carbohydrate, 12 g fat, 62 mg cholesterol, 587 mg sodium, 476 mg potassium.

Sweet-and-Sour Chicken Chunks

Open a package of macaroni-and-cheese or lasagna dinner mix, and turn it into a flavor-packed meal.

Saucy Pizza Skillet Dinner

All you need besides this recipe is a tossed salad and breadsticks, and dinner is on the table.

1 7¾-ounce package lasagna dinner mix
3 cups water
1 4-ounce can mushroom stems and pieces
1 3½-ounce package sliced pepperoni
½ of a medium green pepper, sliced into rings
½ cup sliced pitted ripe olives (optional)
¼ cup shredded mozzarella cheese (1 ounce)

◆ If the noodles in the dinner mix are large, break them into bite-size pieces. In a large skillet combine lasagna dinner mix, water, *undrained* mushrooms, pepperoni, and noodles. Bring to boiling, stirring occasionally. Top with green pepper rings.

◆ Reduce heat and simmer, covered, for 10 minutes or till pasta is tender and sauce is of desired consistency. Uncover and sprinkle with olives, if desired, and cheese. Remove from heat and let stand for 1 to 2 minutes or till cheese melts. Serves 4.

Nutrition information per serving: 245 calories, 13 g protein, 17 g carbohydrate, 15 g fat, cholesterol (not available), 958 mg sodium, 158 mg potassium.

Good-Enough-for-Company Ham Bake

Our panel of recipe tasters thought this was a great way to wow your dinner guests.

1 7¼-ounce package macaroni and cheese dinner mix
1½ cups cubed fully cooked ham *or* chopped cooked chicken
1 cup cream-style cottage cheese
½ cup dairy sour cream
1 teaspoon dried minced onion
¼ teaspoon pepper
¼ cup fine dry bread crumbs
1 tablespoon margarine *or* butter, melted
1 teaspoon dried parsley flakes (optional)

◆ Prepare macaroni and cheese mix according to package directions, *except* do not add salt to water. Stir ham or chicken, cottage cheese, sour cream, onion, and pepper into prepared macaroni and cheese. Transfer to a 1½-quart casserole.

◆ Combine bread crumbs, melted margarine or butter, and parsley flakes, if desired. Sprinkle over casserole.

◆ Bake in a 375° oven about 30 minutes or till heated through. Makes 4 servings.

Nutrition information per serving: 510 calories, 33 g protein, 32 g carbohydrate, 27 g fat, 86 mg cholesterol, 3,185 mg sodium, 1,016 mg potassium.

Calzones

Begin with refrigerated piecrusts rather than making your own pastry for this hearty sandwich and elegant appetizer.

Calzones

Break into the flaky piecrust and discover a delicious pizzalike filling.

1   15-ounce package (2 crusts)
    folded refrigerated
    unbaked piecrusts
¾   pound bulk Italian sausage
    or bulk pork sausage
½   cup chopped onion
½   cup chopped green pepper
1   8-ounce can pizza sauce
1   4-ounce can sliced
    mushrooms, drained
¼   cup sliced pitted ripe olives
1   cup shredded mozzarella
    cheese (4 ounces)
2   tablespoons grated
    Parmesan cheese

◆ Let piecrusts stand at room temperature according to package directions.

◆ Meanwhile, for filling, in a large skillet cook the sausage, chopped onion, and chopped green pepper till meat is brown and vegetables are tender. Drain off fat. Stir in pizza sauce, mushrooms, and olives. Set filling aside.

◆ Unfold piecrusts; cut each in half, making 4 semicircles. Spoon *one-fourth* of the filling onto *half* of *each* piecrust semicircle. Sprinkle *each* with ¼ *cup* mozzarella cheese. Moisten pastry edges with water. Carefully lift and fold each piecrust semicircle in half over filling. Seal edges with fingers and then with the tines of a fork.

◆ Place calzones on a greased baking sheet. Brush with water and sprinkle with Parmesan cheese. Cut slits in tops of calzones to allow steam to escape.

◆ Bake in a 375° oven for 25 to 30 minutes or till golden brown. Let stand for 5 minutes on baking sheet before serving. Makes 4 servings.

Note: To freeze calzones, wrap tightly in moisture-vaporproof wrap. Seal, label, and freeze. To reheat, remove moisture-vaporproof wrap and rewrap frozen calzones individually in heavy-duty aluminum foil. Bake in a 375° oven for 45 to 50 minutes or till heated through.

Nutrition information per serving: 759 calories, 22 g protein, 58 g carbohydrate, 47 g fat, 49 mg cholesterol, 1,491 mg sodium, 318 mg potassium.

Salmon-Sour Cream Turnovers

Next time around, try another sour cream dip—maybe one with toasted onion or blue cheese.

1 15-ounce package (2 crusts) folded refrigerated unbaked piecrusts

1 tablespoon all-purpose flour

1 8-ounce container sour cream dip with chives

2 6¾-ounce cans skinless, boneless salmon, drained and flaked

½ cup chopped celery

¼ cup finely chopped green *or* sweet red pepper
Milk

1 teaspoon sesame seed

◆ Let piecrusts stand at room temperature according to package directions.

◆ Meanwhile, in a mixing bowl stir flour into ⅓ *cup* of the sour cream dip. Fold in salmon, celery, and chopped pepper.

◆ Unfold piecrusts and place on a large ungreased baking sheet. Spread *half* of the salmon mixture onto *half* of *each* piecrust to within 1 inch of the edges. Moisten edges with water. Carefully lift and fold piecrusts in half over filling; turn edges under. Seal edges with the tines of a fork. Cut slits in tops of turnovers to allow steam to escape. Brush tops of turnovers with milk, then sprinkle with sesame seed.

◆ Bake in a 375° oven for 25 to 30 minutes or till pastry is golden. Let stand for 5 minutes before removing from baking sheet. Serve with remaining sour cream dip. Makes 4 servings.

Nutrition information per serving: 731 calories, 22 g protein, 52 g carbohydrate, 47 g fat, 59 mg cholesterol, 881 mg sodium, 501 mg potassium.

Whip up a fast-cooking meal using the versatile poultry parts and products you can buy at supermarkets.

Today's cooks who like to serve chicken and turkey have a lot more to choose from than Grandma's old stewing hen. Today's supermarkets are full of timesaving, easy-to-use poultry products. Here is a list of work-saving items you can rely on when you need dinner on the double.

♦

Cut-up chicken pieces have long been a great work-saver. What is especially handy is that you can buy chicken pieces packaged by type. So, if your family likes white meat and not dark, you can opt for a package of chicken breasts. Or, if the kids fight over the drumsticks, you can buy a package to cook along with a whole bird.

♦

Boneless, skinless chicken breasts are ideal for making into rolls or cutting into strips for stir-frys because the work of boning and skinning has been done for you. This product sometimes costs a bit more, but the convenience is worth the expense when time is short.

♦

Turkey breast portions come both cooked and uncooked in fresh or frozen forms. The cooked version can be sliced or cubed for sandwiches, casseroles, or salads. The uncooked portions can be roasted as you would a whole bird.

♦

Turkey breast steaks and slices are pieces cut crosswise from the breast. They come in ½-inch or ¼- to ⅜-inch thicknesses. Because these cuts are so versatile, you can broil, grill, panfry, or micro-cook them.

♦

Turkey breast tenderloin steaks are lengthwise slices from the breast. These long, thin pieces look like fish fillets, and you can quite often substitute them for boneless, skinless chicken breasts.

♦

Other quick-cooking turkey products are ground turkey; turkey sausage, ham, or pastrami; and turkey franks.

Quick-cook your whole meal by broiling chunks of meat and vegetables on a skewer rather than preparing a roast plus a vegetable side dish.

Sausage Kabobs with Onion Sauce

The trick to perfectly cooked kabobs is to leave a little space between the pieces on the skewer so the heat can reach all sides of every piece.

1 16-ounce can whole white potatoes, drained
6 fully cooked bratwurst *or* smoked Polish sausages, cut crosswise into thirds
2 small zucchini *or* yellow summer squash, cut into ½-inch-thick slices
4 slices bacon, finely chopped
¾ cup chopped onion
2 tablespoons all-purpose flour
4 teaspoons sugar
⅛ teaspoon pepper
¾ cup beer
⅓ cup water
¼ cup vinegar

◆ Halve any large potatoes. Using 4 long skewers, alternately thread the meat, zucchini, and potatoes, leaving about ¼ inch between the pieces. Set aside.

◆ For onion sauce, in a saucepan cook chopped bacon and onion till onion is tender but not brown. Stir in flour, sugar, and pepper. Add beer, water, and vinegar. Cook and stir till thickened and bubbly. Cook and stir 1 minute more.

◆ Place kabobs on the unheated rack of broiler pan. Brush with onion sauce. Broil 4 inches from the heat for 4 minutes. Turn and brush with more sauce. Broil 4 to 6 minutes more or till zucchini is crisp-tender. Heat and pass remaining sauce. Makes 4 servings.

Nutrition information per serving: 498 calories, 21 g protein, 26 g carbohydrate, 34 g fat, 75 mg cholesterol, 944 mg sodium, 645 mg potassium.

Peppery Beef Kabobs

Pouring boiling water over the pepper squares saves you the time and work of precooking them before you assemble the kabobs.

1 pound boneless beef sirloin
    steak *or* boneless lamb
¼ cup soy sauce
1 tablespoon sugar
1 tablespoon cooking oil
1 teaspoon bottled minced
    garlic *or* ¼ teaspoon
    garlic powder
½ teaspoon cracked black
    pepper
1 medium sweet green, red,
    or yellow pepper

◆ Cut beef or lamb into 1-inch cubes. For marinade, in a medium bowl stir together soy sauce, sugar, cooking oil, garlic, and cracked pepper. Add meat, stirring to coat. Cover and marinate at room temperature 20 minutes; stir occasionally.

◆ Meanwhile, cut sweet pepper into 1-inch squares. Pour *boiling water* over pepper squares; let stand 1 to 2 minutes. Drain well. Drain meat, reserving marinade.

◆ For kabobs, thread meat alternately with sweet pepper onto four 8- or 9-inch skewers, leaving ¼ inch between pieces.

◆ Place kabobs on the *unheated* rack of a broiler pan. Brush with reserved marinade. Broil kabobs 3 to 4 inches from the heat for 5 minutes. Brush kabobs with marinade. Carefully turn kabobs and brush again with marinade. Broil 6 to 8 minutes more or till meat is of desired doneness. Serves 4.

Nutrition information per serving: 236 calories, 26 g protein, 6 g carbohydrate, 11 g fat, 65 mg cholesterol, 1,095 mg sodium, 443 mg potassium.

Start with already tenderized beef or pork cubed steaks and forgo the work of pounding the meat with a mallet.

Pork Parmigiana

Our variation of the veal classic saves you time and work.

¼ cup all-purpose flour
¼ teaspoon pepper
1 beaten egg
2 tablespoons water
¼ cup grated Parmesan
   cheese
¼ cup fine dry bread crumbs
⅛ teaspoon garlic powder
4 pork *or* beef cubed steaks
   (about 1 pound total)
2 tablespoons cooking oil
1 cup spaghetti sauce
¼ cup sliced pitted ripe olives
½ cup shredded mozzarella
   cheese
   Snipped parsley (optional)
   Grated Parmesan cheese

◆Combine flour and pepper. In a shallow dish combine egg and water. In a separate dish combine ¼ cup Parmesan cheese, bread crumbs, and garlic powder. Dip steaks into flour mixture, then into egg mixture, and finally, into the crumb mixture.

◆In a 12-inch skillet cook steaks in hot oil about 8 minutes or till no pink remains, turning once. Remove steaks from skillet and keep warm. Drain off fat. Stir spaghetti sauce and olives into skillet; heat through.

◆Spoon spaghetti sauce mixture over steaks. Sprinkle with mozzarella cheese; snipped parsley, if desired; and additional Parmesan cheese. Makes 4 servings.

Nutrition information per serving: 468 calories, 37 g protein, 20 g carbohydrate, 26 g fat, 166 mg cholesterol, 859 mg sodium, 625 mg potassium.

Steak Roll-Ups with Cream Sauce

1 cup sliced mushrooms
¼ cup sliced green onion
1 tablespoon margarine *or*
   butter
2 tablespoons Dijon-style
   mustard
4 beef *or* pork cubed steaks
   (about 1 pound total)
1 tablespoon cooking oil
⅔ cup whipping cream
¼ teaspoon coarsely cracked
   pepper
¼ teaspoon dried tarragon,
   crushed

◆In large skillet over medium heat cook mushrooms and onion in margarine or butter till tender. Cool slightly. Remove with slotted spoon, leaving any remaining margarine in skillet. Spread mustard over cubed steaks. Spoon mushrooms into center of steaks. Roll up and secure with wooden toothpicks.

◆Reheat the large skillet over medium-high heat. Add oil. Cook beef rolls, uncovered, in hot oil for 8 to 10 minutes, or till no pink remains; turn frequently. Remove beef rolls from skillet, reserving drippings in skillet. Keep rolls warm.

◆For sauce, stir cream, pepper, and tarragon into drippings in skillet. Bring to boiling. Boil about 2 minutes or till slightly thickened. Serve sauce over beef rolls. Makes 4 servings.

Nutrition information per serving: 379 calories, 25 g protein, 2 g carbohydrate, 29 g fat, 127 mg cholesterol, 309 mg sodium, 359 mg potassium.

No
More
Pounding

Pork Parmigiana

Skip a step and save washing a pan—cook your pasta and sauce together in a single saucepan or dish.

One-Pot Goulash

This tasty version of goulash features the traditional Hungarian seasoning of paprika but shortcuts the cooking time.

1 pound boneless beef round steak, thinly sliced into bite-size strips*
1 tablespoon cooking oil
½ cup chopped onion
1 clove garlic, minced
1 28-ounce can tomatoes, cut up
1 cup water
1 tablespoon paprika
½ teaspoon dried thyme, crushed
¼ teaspoon salt
¼ teaspoon pepper
5 ounces medium noodles (3½ cups)
2 tablespoons all-purpose flour
1 8-ounce carton dairy sour cream

◆ In a large saucepan cook *half* the meat in hot oil till browned; remove from saucepan. Cook remaining meat, the onion, and garlic till meat is browned and onion is tender. Drain off fat. Return all meat to saucepan. Stir in *undrained* tomatoes, water, paprika, thyme, salt, and pepper. Bring to boiling. Add noodles, a few at a time, stirring constantly. Reduce heat and boil gently, uncovered, about 15 minutes or till meat and noodles are tender, stirring frequently.

◆ Stir flour into sour cream; stir into meat mixture. Cook and stir till thickened and bubbly; cook and stir 1 minute more. Makes 4 servings.

*Note: To make slicing the meat easier, place it in the freezer about 45 minutes or till partially frozen. Then, thinly bias-slice the meat across the grain.

Nutrition information per serving: 548 calories, 36 g protein, 42 g carbohydrate, 26 g fat, 140 mg cholesterol, 534 mg sodium, 910 mg potassium.

1 beaten egg
1 cup cream-style cottage cheese
¼ cup grated Parmesan cheese
1 cup loose-pack frozen cut broccoli
1 10¾-ounce can condensed cream of onion soup
¼ cup milk
1 teaspoon Italian seasoning, crushed
¼ teaspoon pepper
½ pound ground raw turkey
6 lasagna noodles
½ cup shredded cheddar cheese (2 ounces)
½ cup boiling water

◆In a small mixing bowl combine egg, cottage cheese, and Parmesan cheese. Set aside. In a colander run cold water over broccoli to partially thaw; drain well. In another bowl combine broccoli, soup, milk, Italian seasoning, and pepper. Set aside.

◆In a skillet cook turkey till no pink remains. Drain, if necessary. Stir drained turkey into soup mixture.

◆Place 2 of the *uncooked* lasagna noodles in a 10x6x2-inch baking dish, breaking to fit if necessary. Layer with *half* the cottage cheese mixture and *one-third* of the soup mixture. Repeat layers of noodles, cottage cheese mixture, and soup mixture. Top with remaining noodles and remaining soup mixture. Sprinkle with cheddar cheese.

◆Slowly pour boiling water all around the inside edge of the dish. Cover tightly with foil. Bake in a 350° oven for 60 minutes or till pasta is just tender. Let stand, covered, for 10 to 15 minutes or till excess liquid is absorbed. Makes 6 servings.

Nutrition information per serving: 293 calories, 23 g protein, 23 g carbohydrate, 12 g fat, 112 mg cholesterol, 716 mg sodium, 280 mg potassium.

No-fuss layering
What makes this lasagna so easy is that you don't have to cook the noodles ahead. That means there are no extra pans to wash, and layering is a breeze. Just start with two uncooked noodles, breaking them, if necessary, to fit the dish. Then, add cottage cheese and soup layers. Repeat the three layers once more. Finally, add one more layer of noodles and another of soup. Top everything with cheddar cheese.

Dress up a jar of brown or mushroom gravy to create the seasoned sauce for these shortcut main dishes.

Saucy Oriental-Style Burgers

The best of two worlds—hearty burgers from the West and subtle seasonings from the East.

1 pound ground beef
1 12-ounce jar mushroom *or* brown gravy (1¼ cups)
3 tablespoons soy sauce
2 tablespoons orange juice
1 teaspoon ground ginger
¼ teaspoon garlic powder
1 small onion
1 8-ounce can sliced water chestnuts, drained
2 cups frozen crinkle-cut carrots
1 medium sweet red *or* green pepper, cut into 1-inch squares
Hot cooked rice

◆ Shape ground beef into four patties, ½-inch thick. In a large skillet quickly brown patties on both sides. Drain off fat.

◆ Stir in gravy, soy sauce, orange juice, ginger, and garlic powder. Cut onion into thin wedges. Add onion, water chestnuts, carrots, and sweet red or green pepper; bring to boiling. Reduce heat and simmer 15 to 20 minutes or till carrots are tender. Serve with hot cooked rice. Makes 4 servings.

Nutrition information per serving: 456 calories, 24 g protein, 48 g carbohydrate, 18 g fat, 71 mg cholesterol, 1,346 mg sodium, 771 mg potassium.

Primavera Stroganoff Stir-Fry

The frozen vegetable mixture eliminates most of the chopping you expect with a stir-fry, and the jar of gravy makes seasoning a snap.

¾ pound beef top round steak *or* boneless pork
1 12-ounce jar brown *or* mushroom gravy (1¼ cups)
½ cup dairy sour cream
1 4-ounce can sliced mushrooms, drained
1 teaspoon dried dillweed
2 tablespoons cooking oil
½ of a 16-ounce package (2 cups) loose-pack frozen zucchini, carrot, cauliflower, lima beans, and Italian beans
4 green onions, bias-sliced into 1-inch lengths
Hot cooked noodles

◆ Partially freeze meat. Thinly slice into bite-size strips. Set aside. For sauce, stir together gravy, sour cream, mushrooms, dillweed, ¼ teaspoon *salt*, and ¼ teaspoon *pepper*. Set aside.

◆ Preheat a wok or large, heavy skillet over high heat. Add *1 tablespoon* cooking oil. Stir-fry frozen vegetables for 2 minutes. Add green onions and stir-fry 2 minutes more or till vegetables are tender. Remove vegetables from wok. Add remaining oil.

◆ Add the meat to the wok or skillet. Stir-fry for 2 to 3 minutes or till done. Push meat from center of wok or skillet. Stir sauce and add to center of wok. Cook and stir till heated through. Add vegetables to wok or skillet. Stir to coat with sauce. Heat through. Serve over noodles. Makes 4 servings.

Nutrition information per serving: 440 calories, 27 g protein, 33 g carbohydrate, 22 g fat, 75 mg cholesterol, 797 mg sodium, 610 mg potassium.

No-Measure Chicken-Vegetable Soup

This easy soup is so delicious that we predict there'll be no measuring, no mess, no leftovers!

1 14½- *or* 15-ounce can stewed tomatoes with Italian seasoning
2 6-ounce cans hot-style vegetable juice cocktail
1 8-ounce can whole kernel corn
1 small onion, cut into wedges
1 small zucchini *or* yellow summer squash, halved lengthwise and cut into ½-inch-thick slices
1 stalk celery, sliced
2 5- *or* 5½-ounce cans chunk-style chicken

◆ In a large saucepan combine the *undrained* tomatoes, hot-style vegetable juice cocktail, *undrained* corn, onion wedges, zucchini or summer squash, and celery.

◆ Bring mixture to boiling. Reduce heat and simmer, covered, for 10 minutes or till vegetables are tender. Stir in *undrained* chicken. Heat through. Makes 4 servings.

Microwave Directions: In a 2-quart microwave-safe casserole combine *undrained* tomatoes, hot-style vegetable juice cocktail, *undrained* corn, onion wedges, zucchini or summer squash, and celery. Micro-cook, covered, on 100% power (high) for 8 to 10 minutes or till boiling. Stir; cook 8 to 12 minutes longer or till vegetables are tender, stirring once. Stir in *undrained* chicken. Cook 1 to 2 minutes more or till heated through.

Nutrition information per serving: 205 calories, 19 g protein, 21 g carbohydrate, 6 g fat, 44 mg cholesterol, 1,102 mg sodium, 718 mg potassium.

Attention, Microwave Owners!

The microwave timings in this book were tested using countertop microwave ovens with 600 to 700 watts of cooking power. The cooking times are approximate because microwave ovens vary by manufacturer. If you are unsure of the wattage of your oven, test foods at the lowest timing given in the recipes. Then, if an item is not done, increase the cooking time gradually, checking after every 30 seconds.

Need a quick meal idea? Turn to one of the many work- and timesaving fish and seafood products available.

Fish and seafood are the perfect solution to last-minute meal worries because they come in a variety of forms and cook quickly. Use this handy list the next time you want to serve fish or seafood, but aren't sure what to choose.

Whole fish come fresh or frozen. The easiest type to use are dressed fish because they have their organs, scales, heads, tails, and fins removed and are ready to cook. They can be baked, poached, grilled, or micro-cooked.

Fish steaks are crosscut sections from a large fish. Available fresh or frozen, fish steaks are great baked, broiled, poached, grilled, or micro-cooked.

Fish fillets are boneless slices cut lengthwise from the side of the fish. Fresh fillets are easy to bake, broil, poach, grill, and micro-cook. Frozen fish fillets come in blocks as well as individual portions. Because of their thick, rectangular shape, the blocks are difficult to use frozen. But thawed and cut into pieces, the block-style fish are ideal for everything from soups to salads to casseroles.

Breaded and batter-coated fish come in many forms. You can choose fillets, patties, sticks, strips, or chunks.

Seafood such as shrimp, scallops, crab, and lobster can be purchased in many timesaving forms. Although the fresh and frozen options are popular, many supermarket deli departments also have cooked seafood items that save time.

Surimi is the answer if you like seafood, but think twice about the cost. These seafood-flavored fish products usually start with a mild-flavored fish, such as whitefish, that is then shaped and flavored to resemble crab, lobster, scallops, or shrimp. You'll find them most often in the freezer case, but the deli department may carry them, too.

Canned tuna, salmon, shrimp, clams, crab, and lobster are longtime favorites for saving time and work. A relative newcomer is canned boneless, skinless pink salmon. This form saves you the work of removing the skin and bones from regular canned salmon.

Broiled Fish with Mustard-Caper Sauce

4 ¾-inch-thick slices
    French bread
1 tablespoon margarine *or*
    butter
    Garlic powder
1 10-ounce package
    (4 portions) frozen fish
    portions
¼ cup dairy sour cream
2 tablespoons mayonnaise *or*
    salad dressing
1 tablespoon capers, drained
1 tablespoon milk
1 teaspoon lemon juice
½ teaspoon prepared mustard

◆ Spread bread slices with margarine or butter. Sprinkle lightly with garlic powder. Set aside.

◆ Place frozen fish portions on the unheated, greased rack of a broiler pan. Broil 4 inches from the heat for 8 to 10 minutes or till fish flakes easily when tested with a fork; turn fish over once. Place prepared bread slices on broiler rack with fish for the last 1 to 2 minutes of broiling.

◆ Meanwhile, in a small saucepan combine sour cream, mayonnaise or salad dressing, capers, milk, lemon juice, and mustard. Cook and stir over low heat about 2 minutes or just till heated through. *Do not boil.*

◆ Top *each* slice of toasted bread with a fish portion. Spoon sauce over fish. Makes 4 servings.

Nutrition information per serving: 277 calories, 17 g protein, 21 g carbohydrate, 14 g fat, 46 mg cholesterol, 351 mg sodium, 322 mg potassium.

Poached Salmon with Horseradish Sauce

1 tablespoon prepared
    horseradish
1 tablespoon mayonnaise *or*
    salad dressing
1 clove garlic, minced
¼ teaspoon dry mustard
    Dash salt
    Dash pepper
¼ cup whipping cream
2 frozen salmon *or* halibut
    steaks, cut 1 inch thick
    (about 1¼ to 1½ pounds
    total)
1½ cups water
1 teaspoon instant chicken
    bouillon granules

◆ For sauce, in a small bowl combine horseradish, mayonnaise or salad dressing, garlic, mustard, salt, and pepper.

◆ In a small bowl beat whipping cream with a rotary beater till soft peaks form; fold into horseradish mixture. Cover and chill.

◆ Place frozen fish in an ungreased 10-inch skillet. Stir together water and bouillon granules; add to skillet. Bring to boiling. Reduce heat and simmer, covered, for 12 to 18 minutes or till fish flakes easily when tested with a fork.

◆ Transfer fish to a serving platter. Serve sauce with fish. Makes 4 servings.

Nutrition information per serving: 283 calories, 26 g protein, 1 g carbohydrate, 19 g fat, 97 mg cholesterol, 212 mg sodium, 500 mg potassium.

Coiled
Cinnamon Bread

Eliminate the mixing, kneading, and one rising time for yeast breads by starting with a loaf of frozen bread dough.

Coiled Cinnamon Bread

Great for brunch.

½ cup sugar
2 teaspoons ground
  cinnamon
1 16-ounce loaf frozen sweet
  bread dough, thawed
  Powdered Sugar Icing

◆Stir together sugar and cinnamon. Set aside. On a lightly floured surface, roll thawed bread dough into a 16x12-inch rectangle. Brush entire surface lightly with water. Sprinkle sugar mixture over rectangle.

◆Cut dough lengthwise into six 16x2-inch strips. Roll up *one* strip very loosely and place it, one cut-side down, in the center of a lightly greased 9x1½-inch round baking pan. Coil remaining dough strips loosely around the first rolled strip. Cover; let rise in a warm place till double (45 to 60 minutes).

◆Bake in a 350° oven about 35 minutes or till bread is golden (cover bread with foil the last 10 to 15 minutes to prevent overbrowning, if necessary). Remove from oven. Drizzle warm bread with Powdered Sugar Icing. Makes 12 servings.

Powdered Sugar Icing: In a small bowl combine 1 cup sifted *powdered sugar*, ½ teaspoon *vanilla*, and enough *milk* to make of drizzling consistency. Makes about 1 cup.

Nutrition information per serving: 168 calories, 3 g protein, 35 g carbohydrate, 2 g fat, 2 mg cholesterol, 183 mg sodium, 36 mg potassium.

Coiling the dough
Very loosely roll one dough strip and place it, one cut-side down, in the center of the pan. Then, one dough strip at a time, coil the remaining strips loosely around this center.

Onion Braid

Spectacular homemade breads, such as this one, are a cinch with frozen bread dough.

1½ cups chopped onion
1 teaspoon dried basil, crushed
1 teaspoon paprika
2 tablespoons olive oil *or* cooking oil
1 16-ounce loaf frozen bread dough, thawed
1 egg yolk
1 tablespoon water

◆ In a large skillet cook onion, basil, and paprika in olive oil or cooking oil till onion is tender but not brown. Cool slightly.

◆ On a lightly floured surface roll bread dough into a 15x9-inch rectangle. Cut into three 15x3-inch strips.

◆ Spread *one-third* of the onion mixure down the center of *each* strip. Combine egg yolk and water. Brush some of the egg yolk mixture around edges of *each* dough strip. Fold *each* strip in half lengthwise; seal the side and ends well.

◆ Line up the three onion-filled strips, 1 inch apart, on a greased baking sheet (lay them seam side down). Starting in the middle, braid by bringing left strip *underneath* center strip; lay it down. Then bring right strip under new center strip; lay it down. Repeat to end. On the other end, braid by bringing outside strips alternately *over* center strip. (Braid the strips loosely so the bread has room to expand.) Pinch both ends together and tuck under braid to seal.

◆ Cover and let rise in a warm place till almost double (30 to 45 minutes). Brush with remaining egg yolk mixture.

◆ Bake in a 350° oven about 25 minutes or till golden. Cool on a wire rack. Serve slightly warm. Makes 20 servings.

Nutrition information per serving: 81 calories, 2 g protein, 11 g carbohydrate, 3 g fat, 14 mg cholesterol, 136 mg sodium, 36 mg potassium.

Raise your favorite yeast bread doughs six times faster than the normal time with the help of your microwave oven.

If you've always thought there was no time in your schedule for making yeast breads, now you may be pleasantly surprised. Your microwave oven can help you trim your favorite yeast bread loaves from an all-day project to one that takes just a few hours.

First, check to see if proofing is recommended in the owner's manual of your microwave oven. Or, test your oven as follows: Place 2 tablespoons cold stick margarine (do not use corn oil margarine) in a custard cup in the center of your oven. Micro-cook, uncovered, on 10% power (low) for 4 minutes. If the margarine doesn't melt completely, you can proof yeast dough in your microwave oven.

If your oven passed the test, here's the next step. Just before you begin kneading the dough, place 3 cups of water in a 4-cup measure. Cook the water on 100% power (high) for 6½ to 8½ minutes or until it boils. Move the measure to the back of the oven. Place the kneaded dough in a greased bowl, turning once. Cover the bowl with waxed paper and place it in the microwave oven with the hot water. Heat the dough and water on 10% power (low) for 13 to 15 minutes or till the dough has almost doubled. Punch the dough down and shape as directed.

Next, place the shaped dough in 8x4x2-inch loaf dishes. Place the dishes in the microwave oven with hot water. Cover the dishes with waxed paper. Heat the loaves on low for 6 to 8 minutes or till they are nearly doubled. (For breads or rolls that are shaped on baking sheets or in muffin cups, you'll have to do the second proofing step conventionally.)

For rich yeast doughs that have eggs and a slightly higher proportion of sugar, proofing times will be slightly longer. Allow 15 to 20 minutes for the first proofing time, and 10 to 14 minutes for the second proofing time.

Liven up canned soups with some strategic additions for delicious soups and stews with homemade flavor.

Shortcut Vegetable Chowder

Super simple, but so good!

1 10¾-ounce can condensed
   cream of potato soup
1½ cups light cream *or* milk
1 teaspoon dried dillweed
¼ teaspoon onion powder
⅛ teaspoon pepper
1 cup loose-pack frozen peas,
   cut broccoli, *or* cut
   asparagus

◆In a medium saucepan stir together soup, cream or milk, dillweed, onion powder, and pepper. Bring to boiling, stirring frequently. Add vegetables; return to boiling. Reduce heat; cover and simmer about 5 minutes or till vegetables are tender. Makes 3 or 4 side-dish servings.

Nutrition information per serving: 251 calories, 5 g protein, 16 g carbohydrate, 19 g fat, 64 mg cholesterol, 685 mg sodium, 258 mg potassium.

Nacho Corn Soup

Team this south-of-the-border-style soup with a sandwich for a spur-of-the-moment meal.

2 cups milk
1 12-ounce can whole kernel
   corn with sweet peppers,
   drained
1 11-ounce can condensed
   nacho cheese soup
1 4-ounce can diced green
   chili peppers, drained
1 tablespoon dried minced
   onion
¼ teaspoon ground cumin
¼ teaspoon dried oregano,
   crushed
   Dash bottled hot pepper
   sauce (optional)
¼ cup crushed tortilla chips

◆In a large saucepan stir together milk, corn, soup, chili peppers, onion, cumin, oregano, and hot pepper sauce, if desired. Cook, stirring frequently, till heated through and bubbly. Top each serving of soup with tortilla chips. Makes 5 or 6 side-dish servings.

Nutrition information per serving: 180 calories, 8 g protein, 24 g carbohydrate, 7 g fat, 7 mg cholesterol, 956 mg sodium, 320 mg potassium.

Look to frozen spinach soufflé as an easy, tasty filling for mushroom or cherry tomato appetizers.

Spinach-Stuffed Mushrooms

1 12-ounce package frozen
    spinach soufflé
¼ cup fine dry Italian-
    seasoned bread crumbs
½ teaspoon dried oregano,
    crushed
24 large fresh mushrooms
    (1½ to 2 inches in
    diameter) *or* 24 large
    cherry tomatoes
2 tablespoons grated
    Parmesan cheese

◆ To thaw frozen soufflé, place package in a plastic bag; seal tightly. Place plastic bag in a bowl of hot water for 15 minutes, changing water twice. Remove thawed soufflé from package. In a small saucepan, stir together thawed soufflé, bread crumbs, and oregano.

◆ Meanwhile, wash and drain mushrooms. Remove stems and discard; reserve caps. (If using cherry tomatoes, cut a small slice off the bottoms so they will sit flat. Cut a thin slice from the tops. With a small melon baller or spoon carefully scoop out centers and discard. Invert to drain well.)

◆ Cook and stir spinach mixture over medium-low heat about 10 minutes or till heated through. Fill mushroom caps or cherry tomatoes with spinach mixture. Sprinkle with Parmesan cheese. Place in a 15x10x1-inch baking pan. Bake, covered, in a 350° oven till heated through (allow 15 to 20 minutes for mushrooms; 10 minutes for tomatoes). Serves 12.

Nutrition information per serving: 48 calories, 3 g protein, 5 g carbohydrate, 2 g fat, cholesterol (not available), 132 mg sodium, 173 mg potassium.

Forget making a sauce—pull out a pouch of frozen vegetables in cheese sauce for these beat-the-clock side dishes.

Broccoli-Cheese Soup

Serve this foolproof cheese soup with a slice of garlic toast.

2 10-ounce packages frozen
   broccoli in cheese sauce
1 cup milk
½ cup shredded carrot
1 teaspoon dried minced
   onion
¼ teaspoon dry mustard
⅛ teaspoon pepper
½ cup dairy sour cream

◆ Cook frozen broccoli in its pouch according to the package directions. Transfer to a medium saucepan.

◆ Stir in milk, shredded carrot, onion, mustard, and pepper. Cook and stir till bubbly. Add sour cream. Cook and stir *just to boiling.* Makes 5 or 6 side-dish servings.

Nutrition information per serving: 126 calories, 5 g protein, 12 g carbohydrate, 7 g fat, 12 mg cholesterol, 477 mg sodium, 344 mg potassium.

Fettuccine with Vegetable-Cheese Sauce

A great side dish for thick, juicy steaks or chops.

1 6-ounce package frozen
   pea pods
4 ounces fettuccine
1 9-ounce package frozen
   broccoli, cauliflower, and
   carrots in cheese sauce
2 tablespoons dry white wine
½ teaspoon dried basil,
   crushed
   Dash pepper

◆ Rinse pea pods under warm water to break apart. Set aside.

◆ Cook fettuccine according to package directions. Drain and return to saucepan. Meanwhile, for sauce, cook the frozen vegetables in their pouch according to package directions. Add cooked vegetables to pasta. Stir in the pea pods, wine, basil, and pepper. Cook and stir just till mixture is heated through. Makes 4 side-dish servings.

Nutrition information per serving: 170 calories, 6 g protein, 29 g carbohydrate, 3 g fat, 27 mg cholesterol, 282 mg sodium, 242 mg potassium.

Freeze single-serving and family-size portions of cooked rice or pasta ahead of time, and you'll save precious minutes during the dinner rush.

One surefire time-saver is to always have cooked rice or pasta on hand when you need it. Impossible? Not if you use your freezer and microwave oven to help you. Here's how to do it. Start by cooking a big batch of rice or pasta; rinse and drain thoroughly.

To freeze single servings of rice or pasta, place ½-cup portions in 6-ounce custard cups. Cover with clear plastic wrap and freeze for several hours. When rice or pasta is firm, remove the servings from the custard cups. Seal them in freezer bags or containers. Label and refreeze for up to 6 months.

For family-size servings (enough for four people), place 2-cup portions of pasta or rice in freezer containers. Seal, label, and freeze for up to 6 months.

To reheat single servings, return the frozen pasta or rice to the custard cups. *Do not add water.* Cover with waxed paper. Micro-cook on 100% power (high) till pasta or rice is heated through using these timings:
　For 1 serving, 1½ to 2 minutes
　For 2 servings, 2 to 2½ minutes
　For 4 servings, 4 to 4½ minutes

For family-size servings, transfer the 2 cups of frozen rice or pasta to a medium microwave-safe bowl or casserole. Add 2 tablespoons *water.* Cover bowl or casserole with waxed paper. Micro-cook rice or pasta on 100% power (high) about 5 minutes or till heated through. Stir once halfway through the cooking time.

Parmesan
Rosettes

Sticky Peach
Pinwheels

Turn easy-to-use refrigerated breadsticks into fresh-from-the-oven sweet or savory rolls for breakfast or dinner.

Sticky Peach Pinwheels

Take your pick. Just about any flavor of preserves makes these rolls irresistible.

⅓ cup peach, apricot, seedless red raspberry, *or* your favorite preserves

1 11-ounce package (8) refrigerated breadsticks

¼ cup miniature semisweet chocolate pieces

◆ In a small saucepan heat and stir preserves till melted. Pour into a 9x1½-inch round baking pan; spread evenly.

◆ Separate, but *do not uncoil*, the refrigerated breadsticks. Arrange coiled dough atop preserves in the baking pan.

◆ Bake in a 375° oven for 15 to 18 minutes or till golden. Immediately invert onto a platter. Sprinkle with the chocolate pieces. Serve warm. Makes 8 servings.

Nutrition information per serving: 162 calories, 4 g protein, 28 g carbohydrate, 4 g fat, 0 mg cholesterol, 235 mg sodium, 53 mg potassium.

Parmesan Rosettes

1 11-ounce package (8) refrigerated breadsticks

3 tablespoons grated Parmesan *or* Romano cheese

½ teaspoon dried Italian seasoning, crushed

¼ teaspoon garlic powder

2 tablespoons milk

◆ Separate breadsticks and uncoil into individual ropes. On a lightly floured surface, roll each rope into a 12-inch-long rope.

◆ Tie each rope in a loose knot, leaving two long ends. Tuck the top end of the rope under roll. Bring bottom end up and tuck into center of roll.

◆ In a shallow dish combine the Parmesan or Romano cheese, Italian seasoning, and garlic powder. Brush top and sides of each rosette with milk. Carefully dip the top and sides of each rosette into the cheese mixture.

◆ Place rosettes 2 to 3 inches apart on an ungreased baking sheet. Bake in a 350° oven about 15 minutes or till golden. Serve warm. Makes 8 servings.

Nutrition information per serving: 114 calories, 4 g protein, 17 g carbohydrate, 3 g fat, 2 mg cholesterol, 279 mg sodium, 35 mg potassium.

Add pizzazz to plain, cooked poultry, fish, burgers, steaks, or chops with these sauces made with four (or fewer) ingredients.

For a tartly sweet chicken or turkey, glaze whole birds or pieces with a mixture of *bottled barbecue sauce* and a tablespoon or two of *orange juice.*

Brush grilled or oven-baked ribs with *French salad dressing* perked up with a dab of *orange marmalade.* Just heat and stir the dressing and marmalade till they are blended.

Stir a teaspoon or so of your favorite *prepared mustard* into a can of *semi-condensed cream of mushroom soup* and you have the perfect topper for roast beef or pork, steaks, or chops.

Heat together a can of *chicken gravy* and a splash of *lemon juice* for an easy dress-up for cooked vegetables, such as cauliflower or broccoli, and fish.

For a quick and creamy vegetable sauce, mix equal parts of *dairy sour cream* and *creamy Italian salad dressing.*

A fluffy horseradish or mustard sauce can be an elegant addition to beef or pork. Fold about 2 tablespoons of *prepared horseradish or Dijon-style mustard* into a cup of *whipped cream.*

With Oriental food try a mixture of ¼ cup *dry mustard,* 2 teaspoons *cooking oil,* and ¼ teaspoon *salt.*

Spruce up poached fish with a combo of melted *margarine or butter* and a little *lemon or lime juice.* If you like, add a thinly sliced green onion or some grated lemon or lime peel.

Orange-Pecan Stir-Fried Vegetables

Next time, try a different frozen vegetable combination.

1 tablespoon cooking oil
1 16-ounce package loose-
    pack frozen cauliflower,
    baby carrots, and pea
    pods
¼ cup broken pecans
2 tablespoons frozen orange
    juice concentrate

◆ Preheat a wok or large skillet over high heat; add cooking oil. Add the frozen vegetables. Stir-fry for 5 to 6 minutes or till vegetables are crisp-tender. (Add more oil as necessary during cooking.) Stir in pecans and orange juice concentrate; heat through. Serve immediately. Makes 4 or 5 side-dish servings.

Nutrition information per serving: 122 calories, 4 g protein, 10 g carbohydrate, 9 g fat, 0 mg cholesterol, 28 mg sodium, 324 mg potassium.

Fix-and-Forget Italian Salad

A great make-ahead salad for a summer get-together.

1 16-ounce package loose-
    pack frozen zucchini,
    carrots, cauliflower, lima
    beans, and Italian beans
4 ounces provolone,
    mozzarella, *or* cheddar
    cheese, cubed (1 cup)
¼ cup sliced pitted ripe
    olives
4 green onions, sliced
    (¼ cup)
⅓ cup Italian salad dressing
2 tablespoons grated
    Parmesan cheese

◆ In a large salad bowl toss together *frozen* vegetables, cheese cubes, olives, and onions. Toss with Italian salad dressing. Cover and refrigerate for 8 to 24 hours.

◆ Just before serving, add Parmesan cheese and toss lightly. Makes 5 or 6 side-dish servings.

Nutrition information per serving: 213 calories, 9 g protein, 11 g carbohydrate, 15 g fat, 18 mg cholesterol, 452 mg sodium, 300 mg potassium.

Hash Brown
Potato Salad

Parmesan
Potato Salad

Start with frozen or canned potatoes instead of peeling and cubing fresh potatoes for potato salads.

Parmesan Potato Salad

When you're in the mood to experiment, try a different flavor of creamy salad dressing, such as creamy Italian or buttermilk.

2 16-ounce cans sliced
   potatoes, drained
1 8-ounce can cut green
   beans, drained
1 6-ounce jar marinated
   artichoke hearts,
   drained
½ cup creamy cucumber
   salad dressing
¼ cup grated Parmesan
   cheese
1 cup cherry tomatoes,
   halved
   Lettuce leaves (optional)

◆ In a large salad bowl combine potatoes and green beans. Cut large pieces of artichoke hearts in half; add to potato mixture.

◆ In a small mixing bowl combine salad dressing and Parmesan cheese; add to potato mixture. Toss gently to coat. Cover and chill at least 2 hours. Stir in cherry tomatoes just before serving. Serve on lettuce, if desired. Serves 6 to 8.

Nutrition information per serving: 175 calories, 4 g protein, 17 g carbohydrate, 12 g fat, 3 mg cholesterol, 634 mg sodium, 318 mg potassium.

Hash Brown Potato Salad

This sensational salad proves that really good potato salad doesn't have to be a lot of work.

1 24-ounce package frozen
   hash brown potatoes
   with onion and peppers
3 stalks celery, thinly sliced
1 8-ounce container sour
   cream dip with chives
⅔ cup mayonnaise *or* salad
   dressing
2 tablespoons vinegar
2 tablespoons prepared
   mustard
1 tablespoon sugar
1 teaspoon salt
¼ teaspoon pepper
3 hard-cooked eggs, coarsely
   chopped
   Lettuce leaves
   Celery leaves
   Pimiento strips

◆ In a 3- or 4-quart saucepan cook potatoes with onion and peppers in a large amount of boiling water, covered, 6 to 8 minutes or till potatoes are tender; drain well. In a large bowl combine cooked potatoes and celery. Set aside.

◆ In a small bowl combine sour cream dip, mayonnaise or salad dressing, vinegar, mustard, sugar, salt, and pepper. Add mayonnaise mixture to potato mixture; toss lightly to coat. Gently fold in eggs. Turn into a 2- or 2½-quart moisture- and vaporproof serving container. Cover; chill 4 to 24 hours.

◆ Before serving, place lettuce around the top edge of the container; garnish with celery leaves and pimiento. Serves 12.

Nutrition information per serving: 202 calories, 4 g protein, 13 g carbohydrate, 15 g fat, 84 mg cholesterol, 329 mg sodium, 251 mg potassium.

Forget kneading, rolling out, and cutting biscuits and scones—drop these easy versions from a spoon.

Dill-Cheese Drop Biscuits

2 cups all-purpose flour
1 tablespoon baking powder
1 teaspoon dried dillweed
½ teaspoon cream of tartar
⅓ cup shortening
½ cup shredded cheddar, American, *or* Swiss cheese (2 ounces)
1 cup milk

◆ In a medium mixing bowl stir together flour, baking powder, dillweed, and cream of tartar. Using a pastry blender or two knives, cut in shortening till mixture resembles coarse crumbs. Stir in shredded cheese.

◆ Make a well in the center of the dry ingredients. Add milk all at once. Using a fork, stir just till moistened. Drop dough from a tablespoon onto a greased baking sheet.

◆ Bake in a 450° oven for 10 to 12 minutes or till golden. Remove at once from baking sheet. Serve warm. Makes 12.

Nutrition information per serving: 155 calories, 4 g protein, 17 g carbohydrate, 8 g fat, 6 mg cholesterol, 115 mg sodium, 60 mg potassium.

Drop Scones

½ cup currants
1½ cups all-purpose flour
¼ cup sugar
2 teaspoons baking powder
⅛ teaspoon salt
¼ cup margarine *or* butter
1 beaten egg
1 cup dairy sour cream
1 tablespoon sugar
⅛ teaspoon ground cinnamon

◆ In a small bowl pour enough hot *water* over currants to cover. Let stand for 5 minutes. Drain well and set aside.

◆ Meanwhile, in a large mixing bowl stir together flour, the ¼ cup sugar, baking powder, and salt. Using a pastry blender or two knives, cut in margarine or butter till mixture resembles coarse crumbs. Add currants; toss till combined. Make a well in the center of the dry ingredients.

◆ In a small mixing bowl stir together egg and sour cream; add all at once to dry mixture. Using a fork, stir just till moistened.

◆ Drop dough from a tablespoon, 1 inch apart, on a greased baking sheet. Combine the 1 tablespoon sugar and cinnamon; sprinkle over dough.

◆ Bake in a 400° oven about 15 minutes or till golden. Serve warm. Makes 14 scones.

Nutrition information per serving: 141 calories, 2 g protein, 16 g carbohydrate, 7 g fat, 27 mg cholesterol, 115 mg sodium, 60 mg potassium.

Enjoy baked potatoes just about anytime by trying one of our hurry-up cooking methods and spooning on any of these easy toppers.

For baked potatoes on the double, one of these three timesaving cooking methods should fit the bill.

1) Cut the potatoes in half lengthwise and place them cut side down on a lightly greased baking sheet. Bake in a 425° oven about 35 minutes.

2) Cut the potatoes into quarters lengthwise and place them on a lightly greased baking sheet. Bake in a 425° oven about 30 minutes.

3) To bake potatoes in the microwave oven, prick the potatoes several times with a fork. Arrange on a microwave-safe plate. Cook, uncovered, on 100% power (high) till tender, rearranging once. Allow:
   5 to 7 minutes for 1 potato
   7 to 9 minutes for 2 potatoes
   13 to 16 minutes for 4 potatoes
Let stand 5 minutes.

Score the cut surfaces of potato halves (if you micro-cooked whole potatoes, cut them in half lengthwise) with a crisscross pattern ⅛ inch deep. Serve potatoes with one of the suggestions at right. (Do not use spreads with quartered potatoes.)

Butter Spread: Add one of the following to ½ cup softened margarine or butter:
   2 tablespoons grated Parmesan
      cheese
   2 tablespoons snipped chives
   1 teaspoon dried basil *or*
      savory, crushed, *or* dillweed
   ½ teaspoon dried tarragon, crushed
   2 tablespoons cooked bacon pieces

Sour Cream Spread: Add one of the following to ½ cup dairy sour cream:
   2 tablespoons sliced green onion *or*
      chopped pitted ripe olives
   2 tablespoons crumbled blue cheese
      or crumbled feta cheese
   2 tablespoons shredded cheddar,
      Swiss, *or* Monterey Jack cheese
      with peppers
   1 teaspoon Dijon-style mustard

Cream Cheese Spread: Add one of the following to ½ cup soft-style cream cheese:
   2 tablespoons creamy Italian
      or garlic salad dressing
   2 tablespoons chopped pepperoni
   1 tablespoon chunky-style salsa
   2 tablespoons finely chopped walnuts,
      almonds, pecans, *or* pine nuts

Whip, Freeze, And Serve

Easy Chocolate-Chocolate Chip Ice Cream

Easy Mint-Chocolate Chip Ice Cream

Turn four ingredients into two scrumptious flavors of ice cream. Just whip, freeze, and serve—homemade ice cream can't get any easier.

Easy Chocolate-Chocolate Chip Ice Cream

This ice cream is so rich and creamy your guests will think it came from an ice-cream shop.

2 cups whipping cream
½ of a 14-ounce can
    sweetened condensed
    milk (⅔ cup)
⅔ cup chocolate-flavored
    syrup
¼ of a 12-ounce package
    miniature semisweet
    chocolate pieces (½ cup)

◆ In a large mixer bowl combine cream, sweetened condensed milk, and chocolate syrup. Beat with an electric mixer till soft peaks form (about 10 minutes). Fold in chocolate pieces.

◆ Transfer to an 8x8x2-inch pan. Cover and freeze for at least 6 hours or till firm.

◆ Scoop ice cream into dishes. Makes 10 to 12 servings.

Nutrition information per serving: 320 calories, 3 g protein, 30 g carbohydrate, 23 g fat, 72 mg cholesterol, 54 mg sodium, 194 mg potassium.

Easy Mint-Chocolate Chip Ice Cream: Prepare as above, *except* substitute ¼ cup *green crème de menthe* for the chocolate-flavored syrup.

Nutrition information per serving: 291 calories, 3 g protein, 22 g carbohydrate, 22 g fat, 72 mg cholesterol, 44 mg sodium, 139 mg potassium.

Note: If desired, you can freeze this ice cream in an ice-cream freezer. Use a 2- or 4-quart freezer and freeze according to manufacturer's directions.

Study these cold facts and hot tips for cooking shortcuts you'll use again and again in a variety of recipes from desserts to main dishes.

To quick-chill pasta for salads, drain the cooked pasta and place it in a bowl of ice water. Let stand for 5 minutes. Then drain. Remove any unmelted ice.

◆

Let your freezer help you quick-chill foods such as creamy or gelatin salads, puddings, desserts, or cans of fruit. Just cool them in your freezer for 20 to 30 minutes. Be sure to check the foods often so they don't freeze.

◆

Quick-thaw frozen vegetables or shrimp by placing them in a colander and running hot water over them.

◆

Save thawing and reheating time by freezing foods in small portions. For example, freeze cooled cream and broth soups in ice-cube trays. When the cubes are firm, remove them from the trays and place them in freezer bags. Then thaw only the number of cubes you need. The cubes will thaw and reheat faster than a big block of soup.

◆

Get the jump on chilled main-dish salads or desserts by keeping cans of frequently used fruits, vegetables, and meats on hand in your refrigerator. Then, just mix and serve.

◆

If you love whipped cream, but hate the last-minute hassle, just whip some up. Then spoon or pipe individual servings onto a wax-paper-lined baking sheet. Place the baking sheet in the freezer and freeze the mounds until firm. Transfer them to a freezer bag and store them in the freezer. To serve, place a mound of whipped cream on each serving of dessert and let servings stand at room temperature about 20 minutes or till the whipped cream thaws.

◆

To quick-set gelatin, place the bowl of gelatin mixture in a bowl of ice water, making sure to stir the gelatin as it sets up. *Or,* replace ¾ cup of the water in your recipe with 1¼ cups of ice cubes.

Create company-special fruit desserts in a jiffy by dressing up a loaf of ready-to-use frozen pound cake.

Glazed Pound Cake

The raspberry syrup soaks into the cake and adds color as well as great flavor.

2 cups fresh *or* frozen
   raspberries
1 10¾-ounce frozen loaf
   pound cake, thawed
¼ cup raspberry syrup
3 tablespoons seedless red
   raspberry preserves
   Whipped cream (optional)

◆ If using frozen raspberries, thaw slightly. Before removing cake from the cake pan, prick the cake all over the top with a long-tined fork. Slowly spoon raspberry syrup over pound cake, directing the syrup into the holes. Spread the top of the cake with the raspberry preserves.

◆ Slice and serve the cake immediately with raspberries and whipped cream, if desired. *Or,* cover and chill the cake for 3 to 24 hours. Makes 8 to 10 servings.

Nutrition information per serving: 287 calories, 3 g protein, 32 g carbohydrate, 17 g fat, 79 mg cholesterol, 54 mg sodium, 104 mg potassium.

Pound Cake Torte

Buy the ice-cream topping in a plastic squeeze bottle and drizzle a pretty design on top.

1 cup thinly sliced
   strawberries *or* chopped
   peaches
½ cup strawberry *or* peach
   yogurt
1 10¾-ounce frozen loaf
   pound cake
¼ cup chocolate fudge
   ice-cream topping

◆ Fold the sliced strawberries or chopped peaches into the yogurt. Set aside.

◆ Slice the *frozen* pound cake horizontally into 3 layers. Spread the fruit-yogurt mixture between the cake layers. Spread the ice-cream topping over the top layer. Chill till serving time. Makes 10 servings.

Nutrition information per serving: 170 calories, 3 g protein, 25 g carbohydrate, 6 g fat, 58 mg cholesterol, 116 mg sodium, 112 mg potassium.

Making scrumptious dessert delights is a breeze when you start with convenient frozen puff pastry.

Nutcracker Pastry

The perfect ending to a special meal—serve this elegant dessert with a favorite coffee or tea.

½ of a 17¼-ounce package
   (1 sheet) frozen puff
   pastry
1 slightly beaten egg white
1 teaspoon water
2 teaspoons sugar
⅔ cup packed brown sugar
2 beaten egg yolks
3 tablespoons margarine *or*
   butter, melted
2 tablespoons milk
¼ teaspoon vanilla
1½ cups chopped pecans

◆ Let folded pastry stand at room temperature for 20 minutes to thaw. On a lightly floured surface unfold pastry and roll into a 15x10-inch rectangle. Trim any unfinished edges. Cut rectangle in half lengthwise. Cut off two ¾-inch-wide strips crosswise, then two ¾-inch-wide strips lengthwise from *each* rectangle (see photo *below*). Set the 8 pastry strips aside. Place the 2 rectangles on an ungreased baking sheet. Combine egg white and water; brush over rectangles. Place one pastry strip on top of one edge of a pastry rectangle, *trimming to fit*. Repeat with remaining pastry strips to make a slight rim on each edge of the pastry rectangles. (Use two long strips and two short strips for each rectangle.) Brush strips with egg white mixture, then sprinkle with sugar.

◆ Bake pastry in a 375° oven for 10 minutes. Meanwhile, for filling, in a medium bowl stir together brown sugar, egg yolks, and margarine or butter. Stir in milk and vanilla; stir in pecans.

◆ Carefully, spoon *half* of the filling evenly into each pastry rectangle. Spread filling to strips on edges. Bake about 8 to 10 minutes more or till golden. Makes 16 to 18 servings.

*Nutrition information per serving: 202 calories,
2 g protein, 18 g carbohydrate, 14 g fat, 34 mg cholesterol,
105 mg sodium, 82 mg potassium.*

Preparing the pastry base
Cut two ¾-inch-wide crosswise strips and two ¾-inch-wide lengthwise strips from each pastry rectangle. (For a decorative edge, cut with a fluted pastry wheel.) Fit these strips onto the pastry rectangles, as directed in the recipe, to make a slight rim on each edge.

½ of a 17½-ounce package (1 sheet) frozen puff pastry
1 4-serving-size package *instant* vanilla *or* chocolate pudding mix
1½ cups milk
1 8-ounce carton dairy sour cream
⅓ cup seedless raspberry preserves
1 cup sifted powdered sugar
1 to 2 teaspoons milk
1½ tablespoons chocolate-flavored syrup

◆ Let folded pastry stand at room temperature for 20 minutes to thaw. On a lightly floured surface unfold pastry and roll into a 10-inch square. With a fluted pastry wheel or sharp knife, cut into eight 5x2½-inch rectangles. Arrange pastry rectangles on an ungreased baking sheet. Prick several times with a fork. Bake in a 350° oven about 20 minutes or till golden. Transfer to a wire rack; cool. Split rectangles in half horizontally.

◆ Meanwhile, prepare pudding mix according to package directions, *except* use the 1½ cups milk; beat in sour cream along with the milk. Set pudding aside.

◆ Spread raspberry preserves over bottom halves of pastry rectangles. Top *each* with about ⅓ cup pudding mixture. Top with remaining halves of pastry rectangles.

◆ Combine powdered sugar and enough of the 1 to 2 teaspoons milk to make of drizzling consistency. Spoon over pastry rectangles to glaze. Drizzle chocolate-flavored syrup over glaze. Gently draw a knife through the syrup in several places to make a pretty design, if desired. Chill. Makes 8 servings.

Nutrition information per serving: 348 calories, 5 g protein, 49 g carbohydrate, 16 g fat, 16 mg cholesterol, 234 mg sodium, 149 mg potassium.

Keep these five ingredients on hand, and you can fix this delicious creation any time you get the urge for chocolate.

Chocolate-Peanut-Butter Pudding Cake

The chocolate-peanut-butter mixture starts out on top of the cake batter and ends up a rich pudding hidden below the cake.

1 16-ounce can chocolate-
   flavored syrup
¼ cup water
2 tablespoons peanut butter
1 package 1-layer-size
   devil's food *or* dark fudge
   cake mix
½ cup chopped peanuts
   Ice cream *or* whipped
   cream (optional)

◆ In a small saucepan heat together chocolate syrup, water, and peanut butter till smooth; set aside.

◆ Prepare cake mix according to package directions. Stir in the chopped peanuts. Transfer the cake batter to an ungreased 2-quart casserole. Drizzle the chocolate syrup mixture evenly over the cake batter.

◆ Bake in a 350° oven about 40 minutes or till the cake tests done. Serve warm with ice cream or whipped cream, if desired. Makes 9 servings.

Nutrition information per serving: 372 calories, 7 g protein, 59 g carbohydrate, 15 g fat, 29 mg cholesterol, 189 mg sodium, 292 mg potassium.

Using one of these flavoring ideas, create a cake from a mix that will be special enough for company.

Personalized cakes that fit any occasion or taste are no trouble at all when you start with a two-layer yellow, white, or chocolate cake mix, and one of these delicious additions.

◆

To spice up cakes, add any of these options to the dry cake mix:
  ¾ teaspoon ground cinnamon
  ¾ teaspoon ground ginger
  ½ teaspoon ground allspice
  ¼ teaspoon ground nutmeg

◆

For cakes with a delicate flavor, add one of these with the eggs:
  ½ cup applesauce
  1 tablespoon instant coffee crystals
      (dissolved in the water called
      for in the mix directions)
  1 tablespoon finely shredded orange
      peel
  1 teaspoon maple flavoring
  ½ teaspoon almond extract

◆

If you enjoy pineapple, substitute an equal amount of unsweetened pineapple juice for the water called for in a white or yellow cake mix.

◆

Want a marbled cake? Just add ½ cup chocolate-flavored syrup to *one-third* of the white or yellow cake batter. Pour plain batter into baking pans. Pour the chocolate batter atop plain batter. Swirl the batter gently with a spatula.

◆

For tempting bits and pieces in your cake, stir one of these into the mixed batter:
  1 cup flaked coconut
  ½ cup finely chopped nuts
  ½ cup miniature semisweet chocolate
      pieces
  ½ cup well-drained, chopped
      maraschino cherries

Bring out your blender and a pint of vanilla ice cream, and you're all set to serve up luscious frozen dessert drinks.

After-Dinner Sipper

2 tablespoons white crème de cacao
2 tablespoons green crème de menthe
1 pint vanilla ice cream

◆ In a blender container combine crème de cacao and crème de menthe. Cover and blend till smooth.

◆ Add *half* of the ice cream. Cover; blend till smooth. Add remaining ice cream, *half* at a time; blend mixture till smooth after each addition. Pour sipper into stemmed glasses. Makes 4 (4-ounce) servings.

Nutrition information per serving: 194 calories, 2 g protein, 23 g carbohydrate, 7 g fat, 30 mg cholesterol, 59 mg sodium, 131 mg potassium.

Chocolate-Peanut Sipper: Prepare as above, *except* use 2 tablespoons *creamy peanut butter* and 2 tablespoons *chocolate-flavored syrup* in place of the crème de cacao and crème de menthe. Sprinkle each serving with some of 2 tablespoons *candy-coated chocolate pieces.* Makes 4 (4-ounce) servings.

Nutrition information per serving: 234 calories, 5 g protein, 27 g carbohydrate, 13 g fat, 30 mg cholesterol, 104 mg sodium, 227 mg potassium.

Pineapple-Cheesecake Sipper: Prepare as above, *except* use 1 *undrained* 15-ounce can *crushed pineapple*, chilled, and one 3-ounce package *cream cheese,* cut up in place of the crème de cacao and crème de menthe. Add ¾ cup *milk* with first half of ice cream. Pour into tall glasses. Makes 4 (8-ounce) servings.

Nutrition information per serving: 295 calories, 6 g protein, 35 g carbohydrate, 16 g fat, 57 mg cholesterol, 145 mg sodium, 354 mg potassium.

Banana-Apricot Sipper: Prepare as above, *except* use 2 medium *bananas,* cut up, and one 8-ounce container *apricot yogurt* in place of the crème de cacao and crème de menthe. Add ¼ cup milk with the first half of the ice cream. Pour into tall glasses. Makes 4 (7-ounce) servings.

Nutrition information per serving: 252 calories, 6 g protein, 41 g carbohydrate, 8 g fat, 33 mg cholesterol, 97 mg sodium, 488 mg potassium.

Add frozen fruit and ice cream to the gelatin to help quick-chill this creamy strawberry pie in only 45 minutes.

Mock Parfait Pie

An old-fashioned parfait pie always has fruit, ice cream, and fruit-flavored gelatin. This easy-on-the-cook version has the same down-home good flavor and smooth creaminess.

½ cup water
1 3-ounce package strawberry-flavored gelatin
1 10-ounce package frozen sliced strawberries
¾ cup strawberry ice cream
1 4-ounce container frozen whipped dessert topping, thawed
1 graham cracker crumb pie shell

◆ In a small saucepan bring water to boiling. Add the strawberry-flavored gelatin, stirring till the gelatin dissolves.

◆ In a blender container or food processor bowl combine the frozen strawberries, the strawberry ice cream, and the gelatin mixture. Cover and blend or process till smooth.

◆ Transfer the mixture to a medium mixing bowl. Gently stir in *half* of the whipped dessert topping (refrigerate the remaining half). Spoon the mixture into the graham cracker pie shell. Chill in a freezer for 45 minutes or till set.

◆ Just before serving, garnish with the remaining whipped dessert topping. Store pie in refrigerator. Makes 8 servings.

Nutrition information per serving: 246 calories, 3 g protein, 36 g carbohydrate, 11 g fat, 6 mg cholesterol, 168 mg sodium, 121 mg potassium.

Yummy
Bunny Cookie

Transform a roll of refrigerated cookie dough into the quick-and-easy base for a child's birthday treat or an elegant adult dessert.

Yummy Bunny Cookie

Want to have some fun? Pat the cookie dough into other shapes, such as a big bell for Christmas, a giant pumpkin for Halloween, or a huge heart for Valentine's Day. Just be sure the shape is the same thickness all over, so it will bake evenly.

1 **20-ounce roll refrigerated sugar cookie dough**
⅔ **cup canned strawberry *or* cherry frosting**
⅔ **cup coconut**
   Assorted candies

◆ Cut the cookie roll crosswise into thirds. On the bottom half of a large baking sheet pat 1 portion into a 6-inch circle to form the bunny's head. Position the remaining 2 portions of dough atop head, and pat into 8-inch-long bunny ears.

◆ Bake in a 350° oven for 13 to 15 minutes or till done. Cool for 2 minutes on baking sheet. Transfer to a serving plate or wire rack. Cool about 30 minutes before decorating.

◆ Spread frosting over bunny to about 1 inch from the edges. Sprinkle with coconut. Use candies to decorate as desired.

◆ After serving, store any leftover cookie, covered, at room temperature. Makes 16 to 20 servings.

Nutrition information per serving: 217 calories, 2 g protein, 31 g carbohydrate, 9 g fat, 0 mg cholesterol, 170 mg sodium, 67 mg potassium.

Raspberry Cookie Tarts

When you're in a real pinch for dessert, spoon the raspberry sauce over purchased cheesecake or ice cream.

1 10-ounce package frozen red raspberries *or* strawberries, thawed

2 teaspoons cornstarch

1 17-ounce roll refrigerated oatmeal, sugar, chocolate chip, *or* chocolate cookie dough

2 5-ounce containers vanilla pudding *or* two 4-ounce containers refrigerated vanilla pudding

1 8-ounce carton dairy sour cream

◆ Drain raspberries or strawberries, reserving ⅔ cup syrup. (Add water to make ⅔ cup, if necessary.) Set berries aside. For sauce, in a small saucepan stir reserved syrup into cornstarch. Cook and stir till thickened and bubbly. Cook and stir 2 minutes more. Chill in freezer while preparing tart shells.

◆ For tart shells, cut six ½-inch-thick slices from cookie dough. (Make cookies from remaining dough or refrigerate for another use.) Place 1 dough slice in the bottom of each of six greased 6-ounce custard cups. Press dough with fingertips to cover bottom and 1 inch up sides of the cups. Bake in a 375° oven for 12 to 15 minutes or till lightly browned.

◆ Cool tart shells in cups for 2 minutes; carefully loosen sides and bottom. *Do not remove.* Continue cooling for 15 minutes. Remove from cup and cool thoroughly on a wire rack. Stir together pudding and sour cream; spoon into cooled tart shells.

◆ To serve, stir together sauce and raspberries or strawberries. Spoon sauce over each tart. Makes 6 servings.

Nutrition information per serving: 324 calories, 5 g protein, 44 g carbohydrate, 15 g fat, 22 mg cholesterol, 210 mg sodium, 220 mg potassium.

Fix fabulous mini-flans with ease by substituting caramel ice-cream topping for the traditional caramelized sugar.

Individual Flans

¼ cup caramel ice-cream
      topping
3 beaten eggs
1½ cups milk
¼ cup sugar
1 teaspoon vanilla
1 cup fresh strawberries

◆ Pour *1 tablespoon* of the caramel topping into *each* of four 6-ounce custard cups. Lift and tilt cups to evenly coat the bottom. Set cups in a 9x9x2-inch baking pan.

◆ Combine eggs, milk, sugar, and vanilla; pour into cups. Place pan on oven rack. Pour hot tap water into pan around cups.

◆ Bake in a 325° oven for 45 to 50 minutes or till knife inserted near the centers comes out clean. Loosen edges; invert onto dessert plates. Serve warm or chilled with fruit. Serves 4.

Nutrition information per serving: 225 calories, 9 g protein, 34 g carbohydrate, 6 g fat, 213 mg cholesterol, 139 mg sodium, 327 mg potassium.

To loosen edges
Using a small metal spatula or knife, slip the point of the spatula down sides to let air in, and carefully run spatula around edge to loosen. Invert a dessert plate atop custard cup, then turn over both custard and plate together. Lift off the custard cup.

Reach for containers of refrigerated or canned pudding as the start for these two luscious desserts.

Fresh Fruit Brûlée

Because many glass and ceramic dishes aren't broilerproof, we suggest making this mouth-watering dessert in a metal cake pan.

4 cups fresh strawberries, halved; raspberries; pitted light sweet cherries; blueberries; *or* sliced, peeled peaches
2 4-ounce containers refrigerated vanilla pudding *or* two 5-ounce cans vanilla pudding
½ cup vanilla yogurt
1 tablespoon brown sugar
⅓ cup packed brown sugar

◆ Arrange the fresh fruit evenly in the bottom of a 9x1½-inch round baking pan. Set aside.

◆ In a bowl combine the pudding, yogurt, and the 1 tablespoon brown sugar. Spoon over the fruit. Sieve the ⅓ cup brown sugar evenly over the pudding mixture.

◆ Broil 4 to 5 inches from the heat for 1 to 2 minutes or till the brown sugar begins to melt and turns golden brown. Serve immediately. Makes 6 servings.

Nutrition information per serving: 154 calories, 3 g protein, 32 g carbohydrate, 2 g fat, 6 mg cholesterol, 44 mg sodium, 370 mg potassium.

Chocolate Fluff

A thick-and-rich dessert topping that's ready in 5 minutes!

1 4-ounce container refrigerated chocolate pudding *or* one 5-ounce can chocolate pudding
1 tablespoon crème de cacao, coffee liqueur, white crème de menthe, or milk
1 4-ounce container frozen whipped dessert topping, thawed
Pound cake, angel cake, *or* fresh fruit

◆ In a medium mixing bowl stir together chocolate pudding and liqueur or milk. Fold in dessert topping. Dollop over pound cake, angel cake, or fresh fruit. Makes about 2 cups.

Nutrition information per tablespoon: 35 calories, 0 g protein, 4 g carbohydrate, 2 g fat, 1 mg cholesterol, 11 mg sodium, 11 mg potassium.

Vanilla Fluff: Prepare as directed above, *except* substitute *vanilla pudding* for the chocolate pudding and *orange liqueur* for the crème de cacao or other liqueurs.

Nutrition information per tablespoon: 35 calories, 0 g protein, 4 g carbohydrate, 2 g fat, 1 mg cholesterol, 11 mg sodium, 11 mg potassium.

Index

Keep track of your daily
nutrition needs by using the
information we provide at the
end of each recipe. We've
analyzed the nutritional
content of each recipe serving
for you. When a recipe gives
an ingredient substitution, we
used the first choice in the
analysis. And if it makes a
range of servings (such as 4 to
6), we used the smallest
number. Ingredients listed as
optional weren't included in
the calculations.

Index

Have BETTER HOMES
AND GARDENS® magazine
delivered to your door.
For information, write to:
MR. ROBERT AUSTIN
P.O. BOX 4536
DES MOINES, IA 50336